A Woman
Jesus
Can Teach

A Woman
Jesus
Can Teach

**Lessons from New Testament Women
Help You Make Today's Choices**

by Alice Mathews

To Susan,
Karen,
Kent,
and Cheryl,
four gifts from God
whose integrity challenges me
and whose love sustains me.

A Woman Jesus Can Teach
© 1991 by Alice Mathews. All rights reserved.

Discovery House Publishers is affiliated with
RBC Ministries, Grand Rapids, Michigan.

Discovery House books are distributed to the trade
exclusively by Barbour Publishing, Inc., Uhrichsville, Ohio.

Library of Congress Cataloging-in-Publication Data

Mathews, Alice, 1930—
A woman Jesus can teach: lessons from new testament women
help you make today's choices / by Alice Mathews.
p. cm.

ISBN 0-929239-44-X
ISBN-13 978-0-929239-44-6

1. Women in the Bible. 2. Bible. Stories, English—N.T.
3. Women—Religious life. I. Title.
BS575.M363 1991   225.9'22'082—dc20   91-21583
CIP

Printed in the United States of America

07 08 09 10 11
DP
15 16 17 18 19 20

Contents

Preface
vii

Preface

As a small child in a Detroit Sunday school class, I learned the stories of Jesus—how He walked on water and calmed the sea, how He healed the sick and raised the dead to life again, how He fed hungry people and drove crooked merchants from the temple. Before I could read well enough to find my place in a hymnbook, I had learned to sing

> Fairest Lord Jesus, Ruler of all nature,
> O Thou of God and man the Son:
> Thee will I cherish, Thee will I honor,
> Thou my soul's glory, joy and crown.

The first line made sense to me: Jesus was a tireless miracle-worker who had control over all nature. The second line I only dimly understood, but I was learning that the wonderful human being, Jesus, was also God. The last two lines formed a response to Jesus Christ that even I as a child could feel, though I wasn't clear about what "my soul's glory, joy and crown" meant.

Somewhere in the years that followed I lost sight of the Jesus of the Gospels. His place was taken by a more abstract Christ whose perfections removed Him from my daily grind. Most of the books I read and sermons I heard hovered in the Old Testament or the Epistles. If they swooped over the Gospels, it was only for a quick tour of the twin peaks of the Incarnation and the Substitutionary Atonement of Christ. Everything in between dropped from view. The Jesus of the Gospels was theologized into a neat doctrine sandwiched between God the Father and the Holy Spirit. Though I prayed in Jesus' name daily and took non-Christians on evangelistic tours of Jesus' work of redemption in His death on the cross, I didn't find the person of Jesus particularly relevant to my life.

In 1974 I began a three-year weekly journey through the gospel according to John with a group of collegians in Vienna, Austria. The first part of chapter 1 concerned the Jesus I had studied most: the eternal Word through Whom all things were made. Teaching this put me on comfortably familiar ground. This was the stuff of most of my studies. But as we moved into Jesus' earthly life and ministry, I felt less and less at ease with the Jesus I met in John's gospel. I wanted the collegians in my class to worship this Jesus and give their lives to Him. But He said and did strange things. He sounded rude to His mother. It looked as if He couldn't care less whether the religious leaders liked Him or not. The "gentle Jesus, meek and mild" almost seemed to enjoy riling people and needlessly flaunting conventions.

As a Bible teacher I felt caught between my commitment to honor the integrity of the Scriptures and my desire to cover up the puzzling things in Jesus' life that might offend the new Christians and non-Christians in my class. In the process I had to struggle with my unacknowledged feelings about the kind of person I thought Jesus ought to have been. In the pages of John's gospel I met a Man who didn't behave in the way I thought the disembodied, spiritualized Christ of the Epistles would behave.

That began what has become for me a continuing fascination with Immanuel, God in the flesh, the Jesus who walked the dusty roads and mountain paths of Palestine. When I began work three years ago on this series of studies, first for a class and later for publication, I found myself deeply moved by the words and actions of the God-Man recorded for us by Matthew, Mark, Luke, and John. At times as I have worked on these chapters, I've been overcome by powerful emotions of sadness, of anger, of love, of joy. I've met again and fallen in love with the Savior of the world, who happens to be the Savior of individual women and men. I found a Man filled with compassion for women caught on the barbed wire of life. I've held my breath as He defied convention and took enormous risks to offer hope, new life, or a second chance to women despised and ground down into dust under the feet of thoughtless religious leaders. In the process, I've experienced in a fresh way Peter's descriptive words:

> Though you have not seen him, you love him; and even though you do not see him now, you believe in him and are filled with an inexpressible and glorious joy, for you are receiving the goal of your faith, the salvation of your souls. (1 Peter 1:8–9)

If I could have any wish for those who read this book, it would be that Jesus Christ will step off these pages into your life and grip you with His marvelous, risk-taking love so that you will want nothing more than to follow Him and learn from Him all the days of your life.

Jesus: How to Be a Disciple of the Master Teacher

In 1980 my husband and I moved back to the United States after nearly two decades of overseas missionary service. One of the first things that struck me as we settled into the American version of the Christian community was the strong emphasis on discipling. It seemed that every Christian we met was either discipling a newer Christian or was being discipled by an older Christian.

Younger women approached me and asked me to disciple them. Their requests had the feel of something programmed, cut-and-dried. I hated to admit it, but I didn't have a clue what I was supposed to do. So I listened, asked questions, and read books. I discovered an exploding literature on how to disciple or be discipled.

Much that I found, however, was formula-driven: do these five things in this order and you'll automatically be the growing Christian God wants you to be. These looked neat and efficient, and we Americans like things that way. If we can reduce a process to a formula (preferably one that either alliterates or forms an acronym!), we can convince ourselves that we have the process under control.

In many areas of life that works. Formulas do get some processes under control. Every recipe is a formula: take these ingredients in these proportions and combine them in this way and voilà!—cornbread or pot roast or chocolate mousse. Any woman who walks into her kitchen to prepare a meal works with formulas. She either already knows them in her head or knows where to find the ones she will use. If we've been at the business of cooking very long, we don't need to reach for a recipe book every time we make a cream sauce or pie crust.

To learn to cook well, we start out following the formulas (recipes) carefully. As we become more skilled, we may alter the formulas to our own taste. But whether we have five well-used recipe books open on the counter every time we prepare a meal or we work out of cooking experiences accumulated over the years, we are combining certain ingredients in certain proportions in a certain way. We're using formulas. Good cooks and bad cooks alike use formulas. They merely differ either in the formulas they use or in the ways they use them.

Is discipleship the same as cooking? Can I be guaranteed that if I combine certain ingredients (joining a Bible study group, spending a specified amount of time each day in prayer, attending three church services a week, witnessing to non-Christians on schedule) in certain proportions and in a certain way, I will become a mature Christian?

To find that answer I decided to follow Jesus Christ through the four gospels and look at what the master disciple-maker said to those who followed Him as disciples. What I found was that His contacts with men and women didn't seem to fit any particular formula. He is, in C. S. Lewis's words, "not a tame lion." He never seemed to approach people in the same way twice. He suited His method to each person's unique need.

Jesus went out of His way to encounter a preoccupied

Samaritan woman and engage her in a conversation that brought her and many in her village to faith. Yet He distanced Himself from His own mother to move her to a different relationship to Himself. He tested a Syrophoenician woman by refusing her request as a way of leading her on to great faith, but He lavished unsolicited grace on a widow whose son had died. Sometimes He talked in riddles to those who wanted answers; other times He gave answers to questions people had not asked. He refused to endorse Martha's notion of what Mary should be doing, just as He refused to answer Peter's question about the task He would give John.

I thought of the scores of women I had worked with in Europe. Whether singly or in small and large groups, these women were individuals. Each one brought her own unique life experience, her own fears and dreams, her own baggage to the Christian life. I can buy a dozen eggs and assume that all twelve eggs are pretty much alike and will act the same way in an angelfood cake. I cannot assume that a dozen women stirred together in a Bible study group will act the same way.

Cookie-cutter discipleship programs reminded me of the near-impossibility of two women—one a size 8 and the other a size 18—sharing the same size 13 dress pattern. Without a great many major adjustments to the pattern, neither woman will end up with a wearable dress.

No two of us are the same. Not only do we vary in height, weight, and hair color, we vary in interests, gifts, and skills. Just as Jesus molded His response to individuals around their specific needs, so we learn to follow Jesus as His disciples out of our own individuality.

When I was growing up, people had to know their

sock size. Today we can buy one size that fits all. We don't have to remember sock sizes any more. But following Jesus isn't like buying a pair of socks. One size doesn't fit all.

Instead, it is more like a rug I hooked many years ago. I had seen the picture of that rug in a magazine and could imagine it under our coffee table in the living room. Six feet in diameter, it was a single round flower with scores of oval petals in every shade of blue and green. What struck me was that, while the general contours of the petals were similar, no two petals were alike. If they were close in size, they were completely different in color or shade. It was that variety that gave the rug its vibrancy.

As I watched Jesus reach out and touch individual women and men in the Gospels, I discovered that God always works with originals, not with copies. Who could doubt the originality of Mary of Magdala or of Martha and her sister Mary? Like the petals of my hooked rug, there are no two alike.

This is not to say that Jesus did not have specific goals for those who follow Him. He made six statements that help us recognize His disciples when we see them. Luke records three conditions Jesus laid down for His followers: "If anyone comes to me and does not hate his father and mother, his wife and children, his brothers and sisters—yes, even his own life—he cannot be my disciple" (14:26); "Anyone who does not carry his cross and follow me cannot be my disciple" (14:27); "Any of you who does not give up everything he has cannot be my disciple" (14:33). John then gives us three proofs of a disciple: "If you hold to my teaching, you are really my disciples" (8:31); everyone "will know that you are my disciples if you love one another" (13:35); "bear much fruit, showing yourselves to be my disciples" (15:8).

That's a daunting list of requirements for disciples. It appears that Jesus set the bar higher than any of us can jump on our own. We not only must hold to His teachings, love one another, and bear much fruit; we must give up everything, carry our cross, and make all human relationships secondary to following Jesus. No wonder "many of his disciples turned back and no longer followed him" (John 6:66).

Meeting the requirements of such a list would be nearly impossible if being a disciple were nothing more than a formula, an abstract concept. It's tough to give up everything for an abstraction. But Jesus doesn't ask us to give up anything for an abstraction. He invites us into a relationship that so changes our priorities that what was once important matters much less to us.

The word *disciple* comes from *mathetes*, which means "learner." That's what we are, learners. But we are a special kind of learner. I can study French in school without having a special relationship to the French teacher. But I can't study the Christian life as a disciple without having a special relationship to its founder. This is why discipleship as an abstraction slips and slides out of formulas designed to contain it. Life-changing relationships are dynamic, not static. They are alive.

When Jesus steps out of the pages of Matthew, Mark, Luke, and John and walks into my living room, I have to deal with Him, a person. He's not some misty figure in history. Nor is He just a set of teachings found in the Sermon on the Mount. He's alive, and He's dynamically involved in building a relationship with me. I must know who He is and what He wants from me. More than factual information about Him, I must also get acquainted with Him and get some feel for what to expect from Him. Because He is alive, not dead, and because He is relating to me, I can't put this relationship in a box or expect it to develop according to some formula.

It's the difference between knowing the mathematical formula and knowing the mathematician. Facts and formulas are static. To bind the edge of my round rug, I can compute the circumference using πd on a Tuesday in May. I can still compute that circumference with the same formula on a Friday in October. Knowing the mathematician is not at all the same.

What difference does that make? Does a relationship do something for us that facts in a formula fail to do? Great relationships have several characteristics in common. The first is that we take an interest in what interests our friend. What matters to her suddenly matters very much to us. We discover that we have a curiosity about things our friend likes that we hadn't given any thought to in the past.

Another characteristic of a great relationship is strong affection. We take such delight in our friend that we want to spend as much time as possible with her. Our hearts are knit together in love. That is a bond more powerful than any demands either of us may put on the relationship.

A third characteristic of a great relationship is trust. We go out of our way to be worthy of our friend's trust, and we give trust. This is, of all the characteristics of a great relationship, the most fragile. Trust is slow to build and quick to be shattered. But when it is present, it forms a sturdy bridge over which we can haul anything.

When we get to know Jesus and find Him completely

trustworthy, we discover that we can hold to His teachings. When we have accepted that we are loved by Him without any strings attached, it is easier to love others. When what matters to Him matters to us, we won't even notice when other relationships and all that we possess take a secondary place in our lives.

What looked like a bar set impossibly high turns out to be not a bar at all. It is a gateway to joyful service for our Savior and Lord, Jesus Christ.

There is no such thing as discipleship in the abstract. There are only disciples, individual men and women whom Jesus has found and whose lives He is changing. Jesus works with people, not concepts.

This book is not about six principles of discipleship. It's about women whom Jesus encountered. He found them on a well curb, in a temple court, in the market-place, outside a city gate. They were ordinary people meeting an extraordinary person. They followed Him, and life was never the same for them again.

These are case studies of women in the Gospels who met someone who changed their lives by His interest in them, His unconditional love, His trustworthiness. His love enabled a sinful woman to show great love. His interest prompted a woman of Samaria to bear much fruit. His trustworthiness stimulated Mary of Magdala to give up everything and follow her deliverer.

What looks difficult, even impossible in the abstract becomes spontaneously possible, even easy when we move into a relationship of love and trust with God the Son. This book is for and about women who want to love and serve Jesus Christ, who want to be His disciples.

Questions for personal reflection or group discussion:

1. How do you feel about the characteristics of a disciple as Jesus stated them?
2. Which one do you think would be most difficult for you?
3. In what ways does a relationship change the way you might look at these characteristics?
4. How do you feel about your own originality or uniqueness as a follower of Jesus Christ?

Mary: How to Relate to the Family of Faith

With our four children now in their thirties, Randall and I have gone through the tough transitions of learning to relate to our kids as adults. We can no longer be responsible for them. We don't choose their toys, their diets, their clothes, or their friends. Whatever influence we may have over them now, it cannot be coercive. They may choose to listen to us because they honor us or because we have an expertise they want to learn. But listening to us is their choice, not our right. This calls for an interesting shift in the way we talk to each other and in the expectations we have.

These relationship shifts in the family can create tension for all of us. As parents we know in our heads we need to let go and encourage our children's independence. Doing it consistently is another thing. We feel responsible, and our protective instincts get in the way of what we know in our heads we must do.

During such times we may feel as if we're tiptoeing through a minefield. But the transitions we make as our children mature into adulthood are insignificant compared to the transition made by a woman we meet in the Gospels. Her name is Mary, the mother of our Lord Jesus Christ.

We're familiar with the dramatic story of her terrifying encounter with an angel, Gabriel, in which she agreed to become the mother of the Messiah. We know the story of Jesus' inconvenient birth in a Bethlehem stable. We've heard about the adoring shepherds and their story of a sky full of angels announcing Jesus' birth. We somehow assume that a woman bringing such a special baby into the world would be spared some of the anguish we ordinary parents face.

Yet Mary faced an even tougher transition than you and I face as our children mature. She had to learn to relate in a new way to her son, Jesus, not just as an adult, but as God. Her role as mother had to give way to a new role as disciple or follower of Jesus Christ. The things that happened to shift her to discipleship were so important that all four Gospel writers give us bits and pieces of the story. One particularly painful incident is reported by Matthew, Mark, and Luke. Here is Mark's version:

> Then Jesus entered a house, and again a crowd gathered, so that he and his disciples were not even able to eat. When his family heard about this, they went to take charge of him, for they said, "He is out of his mind." (3:20–21)

It started with the rumors the folks in Nazareth kept hearing about Jesus. Some people were saying He was out of His mind. Others said He did His work through the power of Beelzebub, the prince of demons. Still others simply said He wasn't getting enough rest nor even time to eat. Mary and her sons agreed that Jesus would kill Himself if someone didn't take charge of Him.

They talked it over in the family and decided to bring Him back to Nazareth. They would keep Him out of the public eye for a while and make sure He got enough sleep and ate at the proper times. So they set out for the village where He was teaching.

Their concern for Jesus' health was not misplaced. Needy people seeking His touch on their lives crowded Him wherever He went. Men and women in their desperation and pain pressed Him on every side. He and His disciples tried to retreat from the pushing throngs, but even in a private home they were so mobbed, they were not able to eat. Mark's account resumes in verses 31 through 35:

> Then Jesus' mother and brothers arrived. Standing outside, they sent someone in to call him. A crowd was sitting around him, and they told him, "Your mother and brothers are outside looking for you."
> "Who are my mother and my brothers?" he asked. Then he looked at those seated in a circle around him and said, "Here are my mother and my brothers! Whoever does God's will is my brother and sister and mother."

"Who are my mother and brothers?" What a question to ask! What must Mary have felt in that moment? After all those years of caring for this growing boy, to be rejected in this way? She had risked her reputation to bring Him into the world. She had worked tirelessly during His boyhood to train Him responsibly. Now as she heard Him ask, "Who is my mother?" she was forced to recognize that for Him, the physical ties of family were not as strong as she had thought.

Of all human relationships, few reach deeper than the tie of a mother to her child. When we become mothers, we become partners with God in creation, in bringing a new life into the world. Could any other bond be stronger than that?

Mary was fully human. She must have struggled with the humiliation of this rejection. If we walked slowly back to Nazareth with her after that painful encounter, we might see her close her eyes and shake her head as if to blot out this new reality. It couldn't be true. This special son, the one the angel had said would be great and would be called the Son of the Most High, who would occupy the throne of His father David— surely this son wouldn't turn His back on His own mother!

But what had that old man Simeon said to her that day in the Jerusalem temple where she and Joseph had taken the baby Jesus for His dedication? Hadn't he told her that because of this child a sword would pierce her own soul? Was this what he was talking about? Could anything hurt more than being publicly rejected by her oldest son?

As she walked the dusty path to Nazareth, Mary may have turned over in her mind those exciting early months of her pregnancy spent in the Judean hill country with her cousin Elizabeth. During these three months they were two close friends comparing notes about the infants growing inside their wombs. In hushed voices they combed through their memory of angelic visits. How could it be that God had chosen Mary through whom to keep His promise to Israel?

Then it was time for Mary to return to Nazareth and to deal with the stares and gossip of townsfolk. How difficult it would be to explain to her fiancé, Joseph. What if he refused to believe her story about the angel's visit? But God had convinced Joseph in a dream to risk his own reputation to marry her.

She remembered the heaviness of her pregnancy during that inconvenient trip from Nazareth to Bethlehem. She winced at the memory of the innkeeper's words—"The inn is full. We have no room for anyone else." She felt again the exhaustion of that birth on a pile of straw in a hillside stable. All too soon she and Joseph were bundling up their infant son and making another inconvenient trip, this time southwest to Egypt.

When Joseph had talked of returning to Nazareth after Herod died, she knew she would face townspeople who would never believe her tale of an angel and a virgin birth. She would simply have to grit her teeth and ignore the smirks and rude comments.

But she could do that. After all, she had heard Simeon praising God, "My eyes have seen your salvation, which you have prepared in the sight of all people, a light for revelation to the Gentiles and for glory to your people Israel" (Luke 2:30–32). Mary knew her son was born for greatness. She knew He was sent for the deliverance of Israel. She could ignore the gossips!

Of course, there had been that troubling scene in the temple when Jesus was twelve (Luke 2:41–52). It had felt like a prick of the sword Simeon had predicted would pierce her soul. They had taken Jesus with them on that seventy-mile hike from Nazareth to Jerusalem for the Feast of the Passover. She had felt the excitement of seeing again the City of David, its walls a golden white in the spring sunshine. She had stood in the Court of the Women, awed that God had chosen her people to be a light to the Gentiles. She had thrilled to the pageantry and symbolism of the Passover Feast. Every time she had passed through the temple gates, she had experienced the thrill of being Jewish and being able to worship the God of Israel.

Too soon it had been time to make the long trip back to Nazareth. She relived the panic she had felt that first evening of the trek home when they could not find Jesus among the children in the caravan. She experienced again the pounding heart she'd felt as she and Joseph had bombarded other pilgrims with their frantic questions. Where could Jesus be? Repeating that steep climb, they had retraced their steps to Jerusalem, where they hunted for three long days for their twelve-year-old boy. What relief when they found Him in the temple talking with the teachers of the Law! She remembered the first question out of her mouth: "Son, why have you treated us like this? Your father and I have been anxiously searching for you!"

It was His answer that had pricked her. "Why were you searching for me? Didn't you know that I must be about my Father's business?" What could He have meant by that? Didn't He understand that, as His parents, they had a right to be worried? This son who had given them so much love and joy was, at other times, such a puzzle! They had always taken His obedience for granted. Who was this Father He talked about? When the angel had said He would be called the Son of the Most High, was he telling her that Jesus could never be merely their son?

Then all too soon, the child Jesus was no longer a child. He had left the carpenter's shop in Nazareth and had put on the white robe of a rabbi, a teacher. Now she heard stories trickling back into Nazareth that made the slander she endured during His childhood seem insignificant. People were saying her son was out of His mind! Even her other sons thought it was true.

As Mary trudged down the dusty road to Nazareth from that painful encounter with her firstborn son, she may also have recalled His words to her at that wedding in Cana (John 2:1–11). The wine had run out. When she told Jesus about the bridegroom's embarrassment, He had turned to her, His mother, and had asked, "Woman, what have I to do with you?" That had hurt! She had tried to put it out of her mind at the time. But now came another painful question: "Who is my mother?"

In those moments waiting outside the house where Jesus was teaching, Mary must have felt the full weight of rejection as Jesus answered His own question, "Whoever does God's will is my brother and sister and mother."

Nearing Nazareth, her steps grew heavier as she relived the pain of Jesus' words. If anyone had a claim on Him, surely she did! The difficult path of discipleship for Mary meant laying aside her special relationship to Jesus as His mother and relating to Him in the family of faith through obedience to God. Could Mary the mother become Mary the disciple?

* * *

Simeon had prophesied that a sword would pierce her soul. She felt that sword turn within her again on a black Friday. The long walk from Nazareth to Jerusalem for the Passover feast had been exhausting. When she saw Jesus teaching in the temple, she thought He seemed so old, so tired, so discouraged. Wherever He went, people rushed out to see Him, to hear Him, or to watch Him heal the sick. But always the religious leaders of the nation opposed Him.

As Mary stood at the foot of a Roman cross that black Friday, she thought again of this son who seemed to choose a collision course with the religious authorities. The rumors had never stopped. It seemed that He was always saying something controversial or doing something on a Sabbath that upset the priests and Pharisees. He actually seemed to prefer the Sabbath to heal the sick! Did He have to drive the money changers and swindlers out of the temple courtyard with a whip? Did He have to say such inflammatory things to the Pharisees? If only He had seen the importance of staying on the right side of people in power.

Mary thought again of that day when she and her other sons had gone to take Jesus home. If only He had gone with them then! This terrible moment of crucifixion might have been avoided!

Sometimes crouching against nearby rocks for support, sometimes leaning on the other women from Galilee, she watched helplessly as her firstborn son grew weaker and weaker. What more cruel way to die than this? She forced herself to look at that human body—a body once carried within her own body—now suspended between heaven and earth by two spikes driven through His hands into a crossbeam. She tried to breathe for Him even as she watched Him slowly suffocate.

What had happened to the promise of the angel Gabriel that her son would be "great and would be called the Son of the Most High"? How could everything end this way when the angel had spoken such exalted words to her so many years before?

As she stood there, lost in her grief, she heard Jesus

speak to her from the cross. His voice was weak: "Dear woman, here is your son." Then to John He said, "Here is your mother." Not long after that, He cried out, "It is finished!" and her son was gone. Yet in those last moments before His death, Mary was warmed by her son's love wrapped around her against the cold wind and dark skies. In that moment of losing her son Jesus, Mary gained a new family. John the beloved disciple, took her to his house to comfort her and care for her.

"Who is my mother? Whoever does God's will is my brother and sister and mother." Mary had lived with a tension throughout Jesus' earthly ministry, a tension between ties to her physical family and ties to the family of faith. Now, at the foot of the cross, the two roles were brought together into one. Jesus' gift to her in those last moments before His death was to restore her role as mother in a new context.

We meet Mary one more time in the Bible. The story picks up in Acts 1:12–15. Jesus had just ascended into heaven.

> Then [the disciples] returned to Jerusalem from the hill called the Mount of Olives, a Sabbath day's walk from the city. When they arrived, they went upstairs to the room where they were staying. Those present were Peter, John, James and Andrew; Philip and Thomas, Bartholomew and Matthew; James son of Alphaeus and Simon the Zealot, and Judas son of James. They all joined together constantly in prayer, along with the women and *Mary the mother of Jesus*, and with his brothers (emphasis added).

Our last glimpse of Mary is in a prayer meeting with

the other followers of Christ. She had made the transition to discipleship. In the process she moved from the fragile ties of a human family to the strong ties of the family of faith.

Unlike Mary, we have no special biological relationship with the Son of God to get in our way. None of us has ever had to travel the rough path Mary had to walk. Even so, we may find ourselves inventing our own ways of relating to Jesus Christ that fall short of God's way.

"Who is my sister? Whoever does God's will is my sister." Nothing less will do. The family of God is a family of faith. Faith means trusting God to do what is best for us as we do what He tells us to do. Our relationship to Jesus Christ begins and moves forward on one basis only: doing God's will. Anything else we substitute for that must be denied.

It is easy for many of us whom God has blessed with families to allow our families to come before our relationship to God. Faced with the anti-family pressures of our culture, we want to turn back the tide of godlessness around us by making a strong family our first priority. Is that wrong? The answer is Yes, when our family becomes our first priority.

Jesus was clear: "If anyone comes to me and does not hate his father and mother, his wife and children, his brothers and sisters—yes, even his own life—he cannot be my disciple" (Luke 14:26).

A strong family is a good goal. But it cannot be our first goal. Commitment to Jesus Christ must come before all other commitments.

An important part of our discipleship as Christian women is to learn how to fuse being a follower of Jesus Christ with being a neighbor, a teacher, a wife, or a friend.

If our focus is on our role as wife and mother instead of our relationship to God, He may need to upset our ideas about priorities. It's tough to discover that what we thought was terribly important doesn't matter to God at all. To help us learn that, God at times turns our lives upside down. When that happens, we may conclude that everything that has given us significance is gone. But when we look again at Mary on that grim day at the foot of a cross, we know that God is at work even in our most devastating moments of loss. Jesus removed from Mary her role as His mother in order to give motherhood back to her in a new context in the family of God.

Roles change. One woman may lose her role as wife through the death of her husband. Another woman loses her role of wife through divorce. Motherhood can be taken through the death of a child. This kind of tough discipleship pulls us up short. Can we at such times know in a deeper way the God who sees our tears?

The essence of discipleship is to learn to know God, to know Him as completely trustworthy, and on that basis, to do His will. As disciples we grow to trust Him to work all things together for our good as we do His will. When we know God in that way, we can trust Him to "establish the work of our hands" (Psalm 90:17).

He may establish us in familiar roles. He may give us fulfilling new roles. But all of our roles are to be played out in the context of God's work and God's family. It is on that foundation that we build everything else.

As disciples, we learn that all of our human relationships take second place to our relationship to our Creator God and Savior, Jesus Christ. The starting point for each of us as followers of Jesus Christ is to let God be

God in our lives. We trust Him and obey Him because He is God.

The good word is that when we do that, God moves into our topsy-turvy world and establishes the work of our hands. He gives us wisdom, a skill for living life wisely. This wisdom may change our values and our priorities, but it also fuses our discipleship to our daily lives in a way that brings contentment, even joy.

Mary survived humiliation. She survived confusion about Jesus and His mission. She survived His death. She lived to see Him raised from death and glorified. She lived to become an integral part of the family of God when she let go of special privilege and took her place as a follower of the Son of God. "Who is my mother? Whoever does God's will is my brother and sister and mother."

Questions for personal reflection or group discussion:

1. Throughout Jesus' earthly ministry Mary lived with a tension between her view of physical family ties and ties to the family of faith. How was that tension resolved for her?
2. In what ways do we as twentieth-century Christian women also live in tension between our physical families and the family of God?
3. What does it mean to "do God's will"?
4. How does doing God's will affect our priorities?

The Woman at the Well: How to Face Your Self "As Is"

Recently a friend asked me to review for class use a videotape on which I had appeared as a panelist. Without much thought, I popped the cassette into the VCR and pushed the buttons to start the tape. My only thought was to critique the content of the discussion. But suddenly I saw myself on the television screen. I stepped closer. As I stood in the den watching me gesture, hearing me talk, listening to me laugh, I was both curious and apprehensive. I realized, standing there, that I had never seen myself on videotape before. Robert Burns once prayed for the gift "to see ourselves as others see us." For the first time that was happening to me. Good grief! So that's what other people put up with when I'm around!

It struck me that when I look in a mirror, I receive immediate visual feedback so that I can instantly change my facial expression to something more pleasant. But the camera caught me "as is." Two hours of "as is."

The Bible tells us about a woman who met a man who knew her "as is." It appeared that He had no reason to know her, much less reason to bother with her. The man was Jesus. When He encountered this woman, their meeting looked like an accident. It wasn't. But that gets ahead of the story.

Despite the good things He did, Jesus kept upsetting the religious status quo. Again and again He crossed swords with the scribes, the Pharisees, and the teachers of the Law. He irritated them when He drove out of the temple all the unscrupulous merchants who were fleecing the poor pilgrims coming to Jerusalem for the Feast of the Passover. But it wasn't yet time to force the issue with these religious leaders. Instead of continuing His work near the Jewish capital in Judea, He decided to return to Galilee to carry on His ministry.

Our story picks up in John 4:1–6:

> The Pharisees heard that Jesus was gaining and baptizing more disciples than John, although in fact it was not Jesus who baptized, but his disciples. When the Lord learned of this, he left Judea and went back once more to Galilee.
>
> Now he had to go through Samaria. So he came to a town in Samaria called Sychar, near the plot of ground Jacob had given to his son Joseph. Jacob's well was there, and Jesus, tired as he was from the journey, sat down by the well. It was about the sixth hour.

The writer John makes a point of geography that is worth exploring. A glance at a map of Palestine in New Testament times shows the province of Galilee in the north, the province of Judea in the south, and the area called Samaria in between. It seems logical that anyone going from Judea to Galilee would have to go through Samaria.

Not necessarily. Most Jews were so unwilling to have any contact with Samaritans that they made a roundabout trip to avoid having to walk on Samaritan soil. From Jerusalem they walked seventeen extra miles east to Jericho, crossed the Jordan River, then trekked north through the province of Perea until they could recross the Jordan and enter Galilee. The route was almost twice as long as the direct road through Samaria.

Jews and Samaritans were bitter enemies, much like Jews and Arabs today. Back in 722 B.C. the Assyrian invaders had captured Syria and then the northern ten tribes of the Israelites. Samaria had been the capital of the northern tribes. The Assyrians followed the same pattern on Jewish soil they had used in all their conquests: they rounded up all the people who could keep a sense of national identity alive—the nobles, the scholars, the soldiers, the wealthy—and transported them to other lands, scattering them out across the empire. Then they brought foreigners into the conquered land to settle it and intermarry with the weaker people left behind. This happened to Samaria seven centuries before Jesus was born. Samaritans were a mixed-breed people.

Several centuries later when exiled Jews were allowed to return to Jerusalem to rebuild their temple, the Samaritans offered to help. But the Jews refused to let anyone who was not racially pure help with this sacred task. The rebuffed Samaritans set up a rival temple on Mount Gerizim near Sychar.

So strong was Jewish hatred of Samaritans that a well-known rabbinical ordinance stated, "Let no Israelite eat one mouthful of anything that is a Samaritan's, for if he eat but a mouthful, he is as if he ate swine's flesh." Strong words! In Luke 9:53 we later find Jesus and His disciples on a different journey trying to cross Samaria, only to be turned away from one village. Samaritans hated Jews as much as Jews hated Samaritans. Yet the Bible tells us that Jesus "had to go through Samaria."

It was a tough walk. The path twisted and turned through the mountains of the central ridge. Tired, Jesus sat on the side of Jacob's well to rest while His disciples went into the nearby town of Sychar to buy food. Sitting there under a sweltering noonday sun, He may have noticed the lone woman coming down the hill with a water jug balanced on her shoulder.

We know very little about this nameless woman except that she had been married five times and was presently living with a man who was not her husband. We don't know what had happened to the five men she had married at one time or another. Some or all of them may have died. Some or all of them may have divorced her.

One thing is clear: if any of her marriages dissolved in divorce, she did not initiate the proceedings. Unlike today, a woman in the first century did not have that right. Only a man could end a marriage by divorce. It was part of the Law of Moses under which both Jews and Samaritans lived. Moses had spelled out the law in Deuteronomy 24:1–4:

> If a man marries a woman who becomes displeasing to him because he finds something indecent about her, and he writes her a certificate of divorce, gives it to her and sends her from his house, and if after she leaves his house she becomes the wife of another man, and her second husband dislikes her and writes her a certificate of divorce, gives it to her and sends her from his house, or if he dies, then her first husband, who

The Woman at the Well

divorced her, is not allowed to marry her again
after she has been defiled. That would be
detestable in the eyes of the LORD.

This complicated law prohibited a man from
remarrying a woman he had previously divorced. The
rabbis had, however, shifted the emphasis from
remarriage and used the passage to decide the basis on
which a man could divorce his wife. They focused on
what it would take for a woman to "become displeasing
to her husband."

The rabbinic school of Shammah took a strict view
and taught that only some action contrary to the rules of
virtue—like adultery—justified divorce. But Shammah's
disciple Hillel taught the opposite: "something indecent
in her" could mean anything that displeased the
husband, like too much salt in the food. So a Jewish man
who wanted to divorce his wife could choose to follow
the teachings of Rabbi Hillel if that suited him.

Who knows what happened to our nameless
woman's five husbands? If she turned out to be a bad
cook—or worse, could not bear sons—or any thing else
that "displeased" her husband, she could be passed from
husband to husband like a bad coin. What must that
have meant for her to have experienced loss or rejection
five times? The pain of loss experienced once is a pain
from which many women never recover. What must it be
to know that pain not once, not twice, but five times?
The sense of failure. The slap at self-esteem. The panic,
wondering what would happen to her next. Being put
out of her husband's house with nothing more than a
scrap of parchment in her hand that would allow her to
marry someone else and try again.

Even worse, a woman in the first century could not compel her husband to give her a certificate of divorce so that she could remarry. This lone woman approaching Jacob's well with a water jug on her shoulder may have struggled with that problem. It was almost impossible for a single woman to survive without the support of a man at that time. If her last husband had refused to give her a certificate of divorce, she may have found herself forced to live with a man she was not free to marry.

Whatever had happened to this woman, Jesus watched her approach the well at noon, the sixth hour, the hottest part of the day. Most women came to the well first thing in the morning or in the evening when it was cooler. Did this woman choose to come for water when she thought no one else would be at the well? Was she attempting to escape the cold stares of townspeople who scorned her? Jesus watched her trudge toward the well, weary with the weight of years of loss or rejection.

As she neared the well, she saw Him sitting there. Who was He? Only women drew water, except for shepherds who watered their sheep. But there were no sheep. This man was clearly no shepherd. He was dressed in the long white robe of a rabbi or teacher.

Even more surprising, He spoke to her: "Will you give me a drink?" To us that simple question is not shocking. But Jesus broke two strong Jewish customs in that moment.

First, a Jewish man did not speak to women in public. If the man were a rabbi or religious teacher, he might not even greet his own wife when passing her on the street. It was a precept of the Jewish moralists that "a man should not salute a woman in a public place, not even his own wife."

The Woman at the Well

Some Pharisees were called "the bruised and bleeding Pharisees" because whenever they saw a woman in public, they shut their eyes. Not surprisingly, they sometimes bumped into walls, injuring themselves. A strange evidence of spirituality! Jesus, however, was not limited by the customs of His day in His approach to women.

The second custom Jesus broke was to drink from a contaminated cup held by a despised Samaritan woman. She was a woman. She was a Samaritan. To make matters worse, she lived with a man to whom she was not married, and that made her unclean. Double jeopardy. The cup was "unclean" twice: because a Samaritan held it and because the woman holding it was unclean.

Any other man at Jacob's well that day would have ignored the Samaritan woman. The barriers of race, religion, sex, character, and social position were too great. But Jesus was different. He had chosen to go to Galilee by way of Samaria. He had chosen this place to rest because a lonely woman needed to hear a word of hope.

"Will you give me a drink?" He asked.

This wary, worldlywise woman countered His question with another question: "You are a Jew and I am a Samaritan woman. How can you ask me for a drink?" (John 4:9).

Her question hung in the air unanswered as Jesus turned His first request inside-out: "If you knew the gift of God and who it is that asks you for a drink, you would have asked him and he would have given you living water" (John 4:10).

What kind of riddle was this? He had asked her for a drink. Then He told her He had "living" water she could ask for. Was this double-talk?

Jesus posed His question to open a conversation. But He also had a different end in view. He wanted to awaken in this woman two things: an awareness of her need and of God's willingness to meet her need. So He told her two things she didn't know. She didn't know "the gift of God," and she didn't know who it was who spoke to her that day.

Standing in the hot sun, bothered by this stranger who broke all the conventions by talking to her, yet intrigued by His offer, she decided to take Him on:

> "Sir," the woman said, "you have nothing to draw with and the well is deep. Where can you get this living water? Are you greater than our father Jacob, who gave us the well and drank from it himself, as did also his sons and his flocks and herds?" (John 4:11–12)

A good series of questions. She could see that Jesus had no way of drawing water from the well. Was He some kind of miracle-worker, greater than the patriarch Jacob, that He could produce living water?

"Living" water was more desirable than other water. It was water from a spring or a fountain, like Perrier. Jacob's well had good water, but it wasn't running or living water. The well was replenished by rain and percolation. It was not fed by an underground spring or stream. It was not "living" water.

Some Bible scholars take this woman to task for interpreting Jesus' words literally. But is this unusual? In John 3 Nicodemus could not understand the new birth, mistaking it for a physical experience. Later in John 4 the disciples mistook Jesus' statement about having food to eat. They interpreted His metaphor as literal food.

"Are you greater than our father Jacob?" the woman asked Jesus. Again He sidestepped her question for the moment. She would get her answer when she had a different perspective and could understand it. Instead He brought her quick mind back to His promise of living water in verses 13 and 14:

> Everyone who drinks this water will be thirsty again, but whoever drinks the water I give him will never thirst. Indeed, the water I give him will become in him a spring of water welling up to eternal life.

She looked at Him sharply. Yes, the first part of what He said was certainly true. Day after day, weary year after weary year, she had carried her water jug from Sychar to the well and back. Anyone who drank that water would be thirsty again. That was clear enough. Wouldn't it be wonderful not to have to come to the well every day? Could this Jewish rabbi deliver on such a promise?

At the heart of Jesus' statement is the fundamental truth that our hearts thirst for something only the eternal God can satisfy. In every one of us lives this nameless longing for what is eternal. Augustine said it well: "Our hearts are restless until they find their rest in Thee, O God." There is a thirst only Jesus Christ can satisfy.

But our Samaritan woman wasn't there yet. She could think only of a supply of water that would relieve her of this daily trip from the village to the well. How could Jesus stimulate a spiritual desire in her mind? To do that,

He had to change the subject. Follow their conversation in John 4:15–19:

> The woman said to him, "Sir, give me this water so that I won't get thirsty and have to keep coming here to draw water."
>
> He told her, "Go, call your husband and come back."
>
> "I have no husband," she replied.
>
> Jesus said to her, "You are right when you say you have no husband. The fact is, you have had five husbands, and the man you now have is not your husband. What you have just said is quite true."
>
> "Sir," the woman said, "I can see that you are a prophet."

Go, call your husband.

I have no husband.

Right! You had five, but now you live with a man who is not your husband.

Oops! Caught "as is."

An interesting conversation. Up to this point Jesus had been talking in a word picture about living water that satisfies so that the one drinking it never thirsts again. But the Samaritan woman couldn't connect with what He was saying. Jesus shifted gears so they would not talk past each other. He became absolutely personal and plain. She didn't recognize it yet, but Jesus had just started giving her living water.

Jesus did not judge her. He didn't insult her. He simply verified that she had told the truth. Yet in that statement He tore away her mask. She stood before Him with her embarrassing secret plainly visible. She

faced herself as He saw her, "as is." We take that first sip
of supernatural living water when we take off our
masks and acknowledge ourselves as we really are.
Commentators criticize our Samaritan woman for
deliberately changing the subject when Jesus started
probing her marital situation. It's possible she was not
being evasive. In verse 9 she referred to Jesus as merely a
Jew. By verse 12 she wondered if He was a Jew greater
than her ancestor Jacob. Now in verses 19 and 20 she has
begun to suspect that He could be a prophet. If so, it was
appropriate to bring up a question that may well have
troubled her:

> Our fathers worshiped on this mountain, but you
> Jews claim that the place where we must worship
> is in Jerusalem.

These two people—the Jewish rabbi and the Samaritan woman—stood talking together in the shadow of the
two great mountains, Ebal and Gerizim, where Samaritans carried on their worship. Acknowledging her past in
the presence of a prophet, she may have faced her need to
bring a sin offering and wondered where to bring it. Her
spiritual anxiety at having her sin exposed may have
pushed her to take her religion seriously.

Jesus made no effort to bring the conversation back
to her many husbands or her present relationship.
Instead, He took her question seriously and answered her
carefully (verses 21–24):

> "Believe me, woman, a time is coming when
> you will worship the Father neither on this
> mountain nor in Jerusalem. You Samaritans

worship what you do not know; we worship what we do know, for salvation is from the Jews. Yet a time is coming and has now come when the true worshipers will worship the Father in spirit and truth, for they are the kind of worshipers the Father seeks. God is a spirit, and his worshipers must worship in spirit and in truth."

The Samaritan woman's question was about external religious worship. Jesus wanted her to understand a different kind of worship, an internal worship. In the process, He didn't exactly answer her question about where to worship. Instead, He led her to a place where her question became irrelevant. In her preoccupation with the place of worship, she had overlooked the object of worship, God. When Jesus answered her that spiritual worship of the Father is what matters, He moved her away from holy mountains and temples and rituals.

The woman said, "I know that Messiah" (called Christ) "is coming. When he comes, he will explain everything to us."
Then Jesus declared, "I who speak to you am he." (John 4:25–26)

Was this possible? God's Messiah wouldn't waste time talking with a broken woman at a well in Samaria! But could she doubt His word? He had told her things about herself that only a prophet of God could know. He had answered her question about worship seriously. She knew she didn't understand everything He had said, but she did know somehow that she could believe His word. In her encounter with Jesus, she made the journey to faith. We know that from her actions. We pick up the story again at verse 27:

> Just then his disciples returned and were surprised to find him talking with a woman. But no one asked, "What do you want?" or "Why are you talking with her?"
>
> Then, leaving her water jar, the woman went back to the town and said to the people, "Come, see a man who told me everything I ever did. Could this be the Christ?" They came out of the town and made their way toward him.

She didn't have it all straight. But she had gotten enough to motivate her to share the good news with others. In verse 39 we learn that "many of the Samaritans from that town believed in him because of the woman's testimony." They urged Jesus to stay and teach them. He did so for two more days and "because of his words many more became believers" (verse 41).

How did this woman's life turn out? We don't know. We do know that Jesus did not condemn her. He simply let her know that He knew her, really knew her down deep inside. In knowing her, He did not despise or condemn her. Jesus discipled the woman at Jacob's well by leading her to accept the facts of her life as they were without covering them up.

The beginning of having our thirst quenched is knowing that we are known by God and can still be accepted by Him. Following Jesus means taking a clear-eyed look at the facts of our lives without glossing them over. There's nothing quite like facing the reality of ourselves to help us see our need for God.

More than twenty years ago two friends—Annabelle

Sandifer and Jeannette Evans—and I worked together to reach women in Paris, France, with the good news of eternal life through Jesus Christ. We organized luncheons, outreach coffees, Bible studies, women's retreats—anything we could think of to share Christ with women.

To broaden our outreach one year we decided to send Christmas luncheon invitations to the mothers of all the students at the prestigious American School of Paris. Among other luncheon responses, we received a reservation card from a Mrs. Parker. None of us knew who she was.

Half an hour before the luncheon began, while the dining room was still empty, I noticed a dramatically-dressed woman enter the room somewhat cautiously. Garbed in a magnificent suit under a sweeping cape, she had completed the visual drama with an enormous fur hat. A bit daunted by her elegance, I put on my friendliest smile and walked across the room to meet her. Yes, this was Mrs. Parker, but it was clear she had second thoughts about coming to the luncheon. She answered my greeting evasively and left me as soon as she could work her way to a nearby window where she stared at Paris traffic in the street below.

The luncheon seemed to go well. Our speaker that noon was a well-known Christian woman—vivacious, sophisticated, the kind of woman I assumed Mrs. Parker would enjoy. But she looked bored. The speaker ended her talk by saying, "If any of you would like to have me pray for you, give me your name and I'll be glad to do so."

That brought Mrs. Parker to life. "Of all the nerve!" she exploded. "Who does she think she is, offering to pray for me?" With that she gathered up her purse and cape and headed for the door. In the postmortem on that luncheon Annabelle, Jeannette, and I talked about Mrs. Parker and her disruptive departure. We were sure we would never see her again.

We were wrong. A few months later we sponsored a women's retreat south of Paris. Edith Schaeffer of L'Abri in Switzerland agreed to speak. More than two hundred reservations poured in. We were thrilled! Then one day a reservation arrived from Mrs. Parker. What would happen this time? Would she embarrass us again?

The retreat began well. The weather was perfect. Edith Schaeffer thrilled her audience again and again with stories of God's work in the lives of all kinds of men and women. But the three of us kept watching for Mrs. Parker, who had not yet arrived.

She walked in during the afternoon session and found a place in the back of the packed meeting room. I watched her for some positive reaction to the speaker, but her face was impassive. When the session ended, Mrs. Parker appeared to avoid our friendly overtures, choosing to leaf through books on the literature table.

Then she spoke to the quiet woman selling books: "My daughter just became a Christian." Marjorie wasn't sure how to respond. "So is my sister in America," Mrs. Parker went on. "She sends me Christian books." Sensing her need to talk about this, Marjorie offered to drive her back to Paris when the retreat ended.

On the trip back to the city, Mrs. Parker talked about religion, Christianity, churches, and some of her bad experiences with Christians when she was young. Marjorie listened, responded, and prayed.

It is hard to imagine two women more different from

each other. Marjorie had come to Paris for physical therapy after being crippled by polio in Central Africa where she served as a missionary. Mrs. Parker lived in the glitziest section of Paris. Two women completely different in style, in values, in goals. Yet between them grew a deep friendship as they talked day after day about what it meant to become a Christian. Two weeks later Mrs. Parker reached out for salvation through Jesus Christ. She joined her daughter and her sisters in the family of God.

One evening at dinner with a French editor and his wife, I mentioned a Mrs. Parker who had recently become a Christian after our women's retreat. Paul leaned forward when I said her name. "Did I hear you say 'Dorian Parker'?" he asked.

"Yes, do you know her?"

"Know her? Everyone in Paris knows her!"

"Then tell me, please, who she is!"

"She is DORIAN, often called the most beautiful woman in the world."

Revlon's first Fire and Ice Girl in the early 50s, she was one of the most photographed women in the world. A premiere model in Paris, she later opened the largest modeling agency in Europe. She married five times and gave birth to five children, but not always children of the men to whom she was married at the time.

Dorian. After enormous success, her life had begun to unravel. Back taxes owed to the French government would soon close down her business. In the cut-throat competition of international modeling, her business partner betrayed her. Her lover, a Spanish count and the father of her younger son, had died in a racing accident.

Her son was on drugs and failing in school. Life was not beautiful.

After three decades of living without much thought for the people she had walked over, she faced herself and didn't like what she saw. She needed help. She needed God. When I first met Dorian, I saw a woman still glamorous in her fifties, a woman who had held the world on her palm and had swung it like a bauble at her wrist. She could be intimidating to other women and still attractive to men. Who could have guessed her inner thirst? Jesus knew and He met her at the well of her life.

When John wrote his account of Jesus' life and ministry, he observed that Jesus knew what is in each of us (John 2:25). He then recorded two stories, one about a Pharisee named Nicodemus (chapter 3), and one about the Samaritan woman (chapter 4). No two people could have been less alike than they. He was a Pharisee, she a woman living in sin. He was a religious leader, she an outcast. He was a Jew, she a Samaritan. He was at the top of the social ladder, while she was at the bottom. Nicodemus visited Jesus at night; Jesus arranged to encounter the woman at midday. Jesus confronted religious Nicodemus with his spiritual need to be born again. He approached this immoral woman with her thirst, a thirst He could fill. Jesus knew what was in Nicodemus and He knew what was in the woman from Samaria.

As with Nicodemus, the Samaritan woman, or Dorian, Jesus Christ meets us where we are. He seeks us and opens a conversation with us. He is, in Francis Thompson's words, the "Hound of Heaven" who pursues us with relentless love. He does so because He sees our need. He knows that our hearts thirst for something only the eternal God can satisfy. He sees the nameless, unsatisfied longing, the vague discontent, the lack, the frustration even before we admit it's there. We are never far from the longing for the eternal that God has put in our souls. It is a thirst only Jesus Christ can satisfy.

Our deepest thirst can never be satisfied until we know God, who is water to parched ground. We can't know God until we see ourselves and see our sin. Yet we may spend a lifetime covering up what we are. We have forgotten, or perhaps we never knew, that we cannot get anywhere with God until we recognize our sin. When we meet Jesus Christ, we discover that He knows us. We can't hide, grab for a mask, or play "Let's Pretend." He knows us deep down inside where we keep our secret file. He has read everything in that file. He knows us. Even more surprising, in spite of knowing us to our core, He loves us.

When we understand that, Jesus can begin giving us living water. He begins quenching our thirst by letting us know that He knows us but we are still accepted by God. That is life-changing, life-sustaining living water.

A first-century much-married woman. A twentieth-century much-married woman. Both let Jesus show them what they had been and what they could become when they were forgiven and wrapped in the warm love of God. Through their witness others came to the Savior. Dorian and the woman at the well. Both drank deeply of the living water and then started telling others, "Come and see!"

The Woman at the Well

Questions for personal reflection or group discussion:

Augustine wrote, "Our hearts are restless until they find their rest in Thee, O God."

1. Have you found that you are never safe from the longing for eternity that God has put in your soul? If so, how have you experienced that longing?
2. What do you have to know in order to have that longing satisfied?
3. Jesus moved the Samaritan woman from a preoccupation with external religion to an inner conviction that He was God's Messiah and the Savior of the world. You, too, must make that journey. What have been some of the signposts along the way as you have traveled that road?
4. What connection do you see between being a member of the family of God and being a messenger to others to bring them into God's family?

Mary and Martha: How to Live Successfully in Two Worlds

When I entered fifth grade, I began studying what was then called "domestic science." By the time I reached high school, the name had changed to "home economics." I understand college course catalogs now label it "human ecology." By any name it was the same: a semester of cooking, a semester of sewing, a semester of cooking, a semester of sewing. You may have found yourself in a similar track.

I'm not sure which I hated most—the cooking or the sewing. At age ten I could not separate eggs neatly or make decent flat-felled seams. I remember mostly that I dreaded the hours spent in the domestic science rooms.

We learned to sew using treadle machines. No electric wizards then. When I stopped recently at a fabric store for a pattern, I glanced at the array of modern sewing machines on display—wonderful electronic computer-ized miracle workers! While I stood there admiring technology in the service of seamstresses, I also noticed one thing that has hardly changed since my first introduction to domestic science fifty years ago. On the front of the sewing machine just above the needle is a dial that adjusts the tension on the thread as the machine sews.

For a strong, firm seam a thread from the spool above and another thread from the bobbin below must interlock smoothly and tightly in the fabric. An experienced seamstress checks the thread tension and makes minute adjustments in setting that dial because she understands how important it is that the tension be regulated properly.

At times as I sew, I accidentally bump that dial. I hear the click-click that tells me I've messed up the delicate balance of upper and lower threads. I know that no seams will be strong and usable until I get the tension adjusted again. Everything else has to stop until I'm satisfied that the threads are interlocking properly.

As I read through Luke 10 recently, I thought about the tension dial on my sewing machine. Luke writes about a dinner party held in a home in Bethany in verses 38–42 (NKJV):

> Now it happened as they went that Jesus entered a certain village; and a certain woman named Martha welcomed him into her house. And she had a sister called Mary, who also sat at Jesus' feet and heard his word. But Martha was distracted with much serving, and she approached him and said, "Lord, do you not care that my sister has left me to serve alone? Therefore, tell her to help me."
>
> And Jesus answered and said to her, "Martha, Martha, you are worried and troubled about many things. But one thing is needed, and Mary has chosen that good part, which will not be taken away from her."

The scene: a hot day at the end of the rainy season as summer was beginning. A whitewashed village on a hillside just two miles east of Jerusalem. The home of Martha who was possibly a well-to-do widow who had taken in her younger sister Mary and younger brother Lazarus.

She welcomes Jesus and His followers to her home in Bethany. She hurries to arrange a comfortable seat for Jesus and then to bring a cool drink to each of her guests. She nods to Mary who fills the basin near the door with water, then takes a towel and begins to wash each guest's feet. Jesus' followers seat themselves around the large room, chatting quietly about events of recent days. Villagers begin to crowd the doorway, anxious to come in and listen to the great Rabbi, Jesus. This is not His first visit to Bethany. The townsfolk have heard some of His surprising stories before. Perhaps he will tell them more. A few edge in and sit down outside the ring of disciples. Martha and Mary also take their places at Jesus' feet. We know that from Luke 10:39—Martha had a sister called Mary who also sat at Jesus' feet and heard His word. Apparently they both took the posture of learners or disciples, sitting at Jesus' feet.

I don't know how long Martha sat there listening to the Lord Jesus. But I have a feeling that if she was anything like me, she sat there that day with a divided mind. After all, here were thirteen men who would be hungry and needed to be fed. What was on hand to feed them? What would it take to get everything ready? Would she need to slip out and run to a few shops for grain or fruit?

I identify with Martha. I know exactly what she was doing as she sat there. First, she made a mental inventory of everything in the pantry. After that, she planned the menu, making sure she didn't overlook anything. Then she made a list in her head of all the tasks that would have to be done. When she had thought everything through, she glanced around the room surreptitiously to see the best route through the crowd to get from where she was sitting into the kitchen. When she had plotted her exit, she could sit there no longer. She had to get busy! After all, she was the hostess. It was her responsibility to meet the needs of her guests. No one would think less of Lazarus or Mary if the meal were not adequate. The blame would land squarely on her. No time to sit and listen to Jesus now. Perhaps after all the work was done.

Once in the kitchen she felt that flush of excitement that comes to many of us when we are about to do something special for someone we really care about. We want everything to be perfect—well, at least as nearly perfect as possible. Our love energizes us. We are exhilarated by the opportunity to show our love for someone special.

Can you see Martha, now in the familiar territory of her kitchen, turning into a whirlwind of activity? First, start the beans and lentils cooking with onions and garlic. Then dress the lamb for roasting. Grind the grain and mix the bread for baking. Then prepare the figs and pomegranates. Get water to mix with the wine. Set the table. Stir the beans and lentils. Turn the lamb on the spit. Start baking the bread.

Glancing out the window at the position of the sun in the sky, Martha suddenly realized it would soon be mealtime and she was far from finished. She may have felt what I feel when I've been carried along on the crest of my enthusiasm only to realize I'm running out of time and I can't finish everything I planned to do. When that happens, I get angry—angry with myself and angry with anyone else who might have made a difference in accomplishing my plans.

I suspect that is what happened to Martha. Suddenly the plans and the work that had started out as pure joy turned sour. Luke tells us in verse 40 that she was distracted by all the preparations she was making. The harder she worked, the more worked up she became.

It was Mary's fault. If Mary had been there to help her, it would have been different.

We all know that feeling, don't we? It's bad enough having everything to do. It's even worse when someone we think should be helping us pull the load lets us down. Our irritation about the unfairness of it all builds to the bursting point.

That's what happened to Martha. She explodes in verse 40: "Lord, do you not care that my sister has left me to serve alone? Therefore tell her to help me."

Interesting, isn't it, that Martha spoke her irritation to Jesus, not to Mary. Perhaps she had already tried unsuccessfully to catch Mary's eye and signal her to get up and help. Or she may have nudged Mary who shook off her nudge and went on listening to Jesus. We all have ways we use to get a message across. We clear our throat. We drum our fingers on the table top. We make attention-getting motions. It irritates us even more when the other person ignores us!

Whatever had already happened, Martha spoke directly to Jesus, accusing Him of not caring about her. She was sure that, if He really cared, He would tell Mary to get up and help her.

I'm intrigued by the way Martha linked Jesus' care for her to His willingness to tell Mary to get busy.

Martha thought she knew just how Jesus should demonstrate His care—by lightening her load.

That is exactly what we see Him doing, though not in the way she expected. In His response we learn much about our discipleship as Christian women:

> Martha, Martha, . . . you are worried and upset about many things, but only one thing is needed. Mary has chosen what is better, and it will not be taken away from her (Luke 10:41).

The problem did not lie in the work Martha was doing. It was her attitude of fretting and worry that created the bad situation. Jesus knew that Martha put too much stress on things that didn't matter. Martha's problem was one of balance, of holding life in the proper tension. Take a closer look at what Jesus said and did not say to this overburdened woman.

First, Jesus did not rebuke her for making preparations for Him and His disciples. If she as the hostess in the home had decided to skip any food preparation, her guests would have gone hungry. What was going on in that Bethany kitchen was important.

Do you recall what Jesus had said to Satan when tempted in the wilderness at the outset of His public ministry? In Matthew 4:4 we read, "Man does not live by bread alone." Jesus did not say, "People don't live by bread." We do live by bread. We have bodies that must be fed. Jesus knew that and fed people—as many as five thousand at one time.

But Jesus also knew that people are more than bodies. We do not live by bread alone. To feed our spirits is at least as important as feeding our bodies. Martha's problem was not that she was preparing food for her guests to eat. That was necessary, and in her role as hostess, it was her place to see that it was done. But she gave it too much importance. Instead of settling for a simple supper, she tried to impress with an elaborate meal. Jesus in essence told her that one dish would have been enough.

We all have responsibilities we carry out every day of our lives. We go to the office. We cook. We grade papers. We clean the house. We do the laundry. We do these things, and we want to do them well. Dorothy Sayers reminds us that no crooked table legs came out of the carpenter shop in Nazareth. God is not honored by shoddy work or the neglect of our necessary duties in life.

But we must be sure that the necessary doesn't get out of proportion and distort our lives. We can easily confuse means and ends. Without thinking, we can turn what is a means to living for God into an end in itself. When we take something that is not too important and make it primary in our lives, what is otherwise harmless can become a stumbling block for us.

One of the things Jesus saw that afternoon two thousand years ago was that Martha was looking down on what Mary had chosen to do. Martha imposed her value system—possibly a sparkling house and certainly a sumptuous meal—on Mary. If bustling around was "necessary" for Martha, it must also be necessary for Mary.

Note that Jesus did not tell Martha to do what Mary was doing. At the same time, He pointed out that Mary had chosen the good part. In saying this, Jesus made a little play on words that does not come through in English translations. In essence He said, "Martha, you are preparing many dishes for us to eat, but Mary has prepared the one dish you can't fix in your kitchen." While food was necessary, something much simpler would have been better, allowing Martha to continue sitting with Mary and learning from Christ.

Do you think Jesus was being a bit hard on Martha? After all, she was doing all this work to please Him! Yet do you think He was pleased with her request that He tell Mary to get up and help her? Do you think Mary was pleased to be humiliated in that way? Do you think the disciples and neighbors were pleased to have the Teacher interrupted in that way? And what about Martha herself? Do you think she was pleased with herself? We know when we have spoiled things for ourselves and others around us. And spoil things Martha did!

As you picture this scene in your mind, what image of Martha comes into your head? Elisabeth Moltmann-Wendel remarked that whenever she thinks of Martha, she remembers a picture from a children's Bible. In it Mary is sitting at Jesus' feet listening and Martha is in the background, leaning against the kitchen door with an evil, mistrustful look on her face.

When we think about these two sisters, we tend to imagine Mary with an aura of holiness around her, and we associate Martha with olive oil and fish.

When someone says, "She's a Martha-type," we know just what that means. Someone who is practical, competent, down-to-earth. Marthas are certainly useful and necessary. The church would be in a tough spot if we were all Marys. But when it comes to painting a model or an ideal, it's Mary all the way. That puts us in a bind of sorts, if we think about it. Martha's work is necessary— in the church and in the home. But Mary gets the halo.

Martha, called the patron saint of housewives and cooks, comes in for quite a bit of bashing. Martin Luther wrote, "Martha, your work must be punished and counted as naught . . . I will have no work but the work of Mary."

Stiff words! So I feel a bit sheepish about being a Martha. But Martin Luther was wrong. Martha's work must not be punished and counted as naught. Martha's attitude needed correcting. Martha's perspective needed changing. But Martha's work is good and necessary. The reality is that as followers of Jesus Christ, we need to cultivate both the Martha and the Mary in each of us.

Earlier in Luke 10 we find the story of a lawyer who tried to trap Jesus by asking Him what he had to do to inherit eternal life. Jesus turned the question back on the lawyer by asking him simply, "What is written in the law? What is your reading of it?" The lawyer responded with that great statement taken from Deuteronomy 6:5 and Leviticus 19:18—we are to love the Lord our God with all our heart, with all our soul, with all our strength, and with all our mind, and our neighbor as ourselves.

The lawyer got the answer absolutely right. Jesus agreed, saying, "You have answered correctly. Do this and you will live."

The lawyer could have left it at that, but he didn't. He pressed Jesus with another question: "And just who is my neighbor?" To answer that, Jesus told one of those wonderful stories that take us by surprise.

The story was about a man traveling from Jerusalem down to Jericho on a dusty mountain road. Some thieves attacked him, stripped him naked, beat him up, and left him half dead. First, a priest came by. He might have just finished his week of service rotation in Jerusalem and was on his way home for another year. He saw this poor man, but went out of his way to avoid any contact with him. Then a Levite came along. Levites in first-century Palestine were a kind of lower-order priest who sang at the time of the sacrifice and who served as a doorkeeper and servant to the higher-order priests. The Levite, like the priest, glanced at the injured man and passed by on the other side of the road.

The third person who came along was a Samaritan, despised by the Jews. You have to know how much Jews detested Samaritans to have any idea how shocking this story was that Jesus would say a Samaritan came along. This despised foreigner saw the man, and, instead of doing what the religious Jews had done, he stopped and dressed and bandaged the poor man's wounds, put the man on his donkey, and took him to an inn where he cared for him. He even paid the innkeeper to continue caring for the man while he went on his way.

What was the punch line? When Jesus finished the story, He asked the lawyer, "Who do you think was a neighbor to the injured man?" Of course, the lawyer had to say, "The one who showed mercy to him." And Jesus answered, "Go and do likewise."

Wasn't that just what Martha had done? Hadn't she inconvenienced herself to treat Jesus and His disciples kindly? Wasn't she meeting someone else's need? Absolutely! Wasn't she being a good Samaritan while Mary ignored the physical needs of their guests as the two religious Jews had ignored the man who was beaten and robbed?

Take a second look at the answer for which Jesus commended that first-century lawyer: we are to love the Lord our God with [from] all our heart, with all our soul, with all our strength, and with all our mind, and our neighbor as ourselves.

Note the order of the two loves: God first, then neighbor. Not the other way around. It is not a question of contrasting the activist life to the contemplative life. It's a matter of priorities. We put listening to and learning the Word of God before service. That equips and inspires us for our service for God to others.

What Jesus wanted that day was not Martha's lentils and lamb, but Martha herself. The one dish she could not prepare in her kitchen was her relationship to God. She could prepare that dish only by remaining at Jesus' feet and letting Him provide the food for her soul.

Martha wanted Jesus to lighten her load that day. He did exactly that, but not the way she thought it should be done. He knew that our relationship with God does not develop in the midst of fretting busyness. The one thing needful is to hear God speak to us. Mary chose to put time into that primary relationship and not to be distracted by trivia.

"Martha must be a Mary," wrote one commentator, "and the true Mary must also be a Martha; both are sisters." That brings me back to my sewing machine tension dial. If the tension on the top thread is too loose, the underside of the fabric will be snarled with excess thread. The seam has no strength. It pulls apart hopelessly the moment pressure is applied to it. The only thing a seamstress can do is to pull out all the threads, adjust the tension, and start over.

We also have no usable seam if the threads are not feeding from both the top spool and the underneath bobbin. We could try to sew all day with only the top spool on the machine and nothing in the bobbin holder.

We would not have a single seam. The Martha thread and the Mary thread must both be properly feeding and interlocking if we are to have any seam at all. The balance between the two has to be finely adjusted if the resulting seam is to be strong and usable.

We live in this world. This means we concern ourselves with food and clothes and homes and family and jobs and studies. But we also live in the world of the spirit. We concern ourselves with our relationship to God. That was Martha's real problem. She was sewing with no thread in the bobbin.

To get our service right, we get our priorities right. We let Jesus minister to us before we go out to minister for Him. That is God's order: we first love the Lord our God with all our heart, soul, strength, and mind, and then we are prepared to go out and love our neighbor as ourselves. When we turn that upside down, we may end up feeling overworked and unappreciated. When we keep our priorities in line with God's priorities, we will find that God enables us to do what needs to be done with joy and satisfaction.

Questions for personal reflection or group discussion:

1. When you think of Mary and Martha, with whom do you naturally identify?
2. What steps could you take to gain a better balance between the priorities of Mary and the priorities of Martha in your life?
3. How does worry affect a woman's relationship to God?
4. What have you learned from Mary and Martha that will affect your discipleship in the future?

Martha and Mary: How to Nourish Hope in Times of Loss

When my husband finished his studies at Denver Seminary in 1956, we moved to his first pastorate in a small town in central Wyoming. As we got acquainted with the leaders of the church, we came to appreciate one older couple in particular. Gene, a retired carpenter, arrived at the church every morning to help build an addition to the church education wing. Mae stopped by almost as often. We admired the tireless commitment to Jesus Christ and to His church they both lived in front of us daily.

About six months after we arrived, a phone call brought the news that Don, Gene's and Mae's only son, had just been crushed to death in a local open-pit mine accident. We hurried across town to be with our friends as they groped through their shock and disbelief. It would be an excruciating time for them as they moved through their grief. But we were sure they would make it. They had all the Christian resources to support them during this crisis. Other friends came in, and we were confident that an entire community would surround them, their daughter-in-law, and two grandsons with love and concern.

A few days after the funeral Gene returned to his volunteer work on the church building. But on Sundays he came to church alone. When we dropped by their house, we sensed that Gene was finding strength to cope with his grief, but it was different for Mae.

When we asked about this, we learned that from the time word of the accident came, Mae turned her back on God. How could she believe in a God who would deny them their only child and deny their grandsons a father? God could not possibly be loving and kind and, at the same time, deal them such a blow. Whenever we visited her, we listened to her case against God. It was clear that the facts of her faith and the facts of her life didn't mesh. The faith that we thought would sustain her seemed to get in her way.

Mae reminded me of two other women who sent for Jesus when their brother was seriously ill. But Jesus didn't arrive in time to help them. When He finally showed up, both women said to Him, "Lord, if you had been here, our brother wouldn't have died!" These sisters had enough faith to believe that if Jesus had come, He could have healed their brother. But it looked as if Jesus had let them down.

The story is found in John 11. The first six verses tell us this:

> Now a man named Lazarus was sick. He was from Bethany, the village of Mary and her sister Martha. This Mary, whose brother Lazarus now lay sick, was the same one who poured perfume on the Lord and wiped his feet with her hair. So the sisters sent word to Jesus, "Lord, the one you love is sick." When he heard this, Jesus said, "This sickness will not end in death. No, it is for God's glory so that God's Son may be glorified through it." Jesus loved Martha and her sister and Lazarus.

Yet when he heard that Lazarus was sick, he stayed where he was two more days.

That's the setting. Lazarus was sick. His two sisters, Mary and Martha, turned at once to their friend Jesus, hoping He would come quickly and heal their brother before it was too late.

Knowing that Jesus loved this trio, we would expect Him to set out immediately for Bethany to do what He could to spare them anxiety and grief. Yet we see Jesus not responding in the way the two sisters hoped. Instead of leaving at once for Bethany, He stayed where He was for two more days.

An important principle in life is that love permits pain. We don't want it that way. We want to believe that if God truly loves us, He will not allow anything painful to invade our lives. But this is not so. God's love does not guarantee us a shelter from difficult experiences that are necessary for our spiritual growth. Love and delay are compatible.

If Jesus had rushed off to Bethany as soon as He received word of Lazarus' illness, Mary and Martha would not have been suspended between hope and despair, hope that the one who could help their brother would arrive in time, despair that He would come too late. They would have been spared the anguish of watching Lazarus sink into death. They would have avoided the agony of those last moments before they closed Lazarus' eyes and prepared his body for burial. They would have forestalled the desolation of bereavement. But Jesus didn't come.

He knew that it was time for Mary, Martha, and His disciples to learn what they could not learn if He intervened too quickly. John 11 tells us how completely in control of the situation Jesus was. He knew just what He was doing. He knew that the spiritual growth of Martha and Mary and His band of disciples traveling with Him depended on the right timing. How do we know that? Read John 11:7–16:

> Then Jesus said to his disciples, "Let us go back to Judea."
>
> "But Rabbi," they said, "a short while ago the Jews tried to stone you, and yet you are going back there?"
>
> Jesus answered, "Are there not twelve hours of daylight? A man who walks by day will not stumble, for he sees by this world's light. It is when he walks by night that he stumbles, for he has no light." After he had said this, he went on to tell them, "Our friend Lazarus has fallen asleep; but I am going there to wake him up."
>
> His disciples replied, "Lord, if he sleeps, he will get better." Jesus had been speaking of his death, but his disciples thought he meant natural sleep.
>
> So then he told them plainly, "Lazarus is dead, and for your sake I am glad I was not there, so that you may believe. But let us go to him."
>
> Then Thomas (called Didymus) said to the rest of the disciples, "Let us also go, that we may die with him."

Divine timing. Jesus knew that Mary and Martha would never know Him as the Resurrection and the Life had Lazarus not died. David would not have known God as his Rock and his Fortress had he not been hunted by

Saul in the mountains of Engedi. The Israelites would not have known God as their Deliverer had they not been slaves in Egypt. Our painful experiences can reveal God to us in new ways. Jesus knew precisely what He was doing.

On His arrival, Jesus found that Lazarus had been in the tomb for four days. Many Jews had come from Jerusalem to Bethany to comfort Martha and Mary in the loss of their brother. Sympathy for them was the first of all duties. Nothing else was more important than expressing sorrow with the bereaved.

In the hot climate of Palestine the deceased had to be buried immediately after death. Women anointed the body with the finest spices and ointments, then wrapped it in a linen garment with the hands and feet swathed in bandage-like wrappings and the head enclosed in a towel. Everyone who could possibly come would join the procession from the house to the tomb. Curiously, women walked first because, according to the teachers of the day, it was a woman by her sin in the Garden of Eden who was responsible for death coming into the world.

At the tomb friends made memorial speeches. Then the mourners formed two long lines between which the family members walked. As long as the dead body remained in the house, the family was forbidden to prepare food there, to eat meat or drink wine, or to study. When the body was carried out, all the furniture was turned upside-down and the mourners sat on the ground or on low stools. On returning from the tomb, they ate a meal of bread, hard-boiled eggs, and lentils, symbolizing life, which was always rolling toward death.

Deep mourning lasted seven days, during which no one could anoint himself, put on shoes, engage in study or business, or even wash. Thirty days of lighter mourning followed the week of heavy mourning.

In the middle of this period of deep mourning, Martha heard that Jesus was entering the village. Violating the conventions of the East, she went out to meet Him while Mary stayed in the house. The gospel writer records the remarkable conversation Martha and Jesus had in John 11:21–27:

> "Lord," Martha said to Jesus, "if you had been here, my brother would not have died. But I know that even now God will give you whatever you ask."
>
> Jesus said to her, "Your brother will rise again."
>
> Martha answered, "I know he will rise again in the resurrection at the last day."
>
> Jesus said to her, "I am the resurrection and the life. He who believes in me will live, even though he dies; and whoever lives and believes in me will never die. Do you believe this?"
>
> "Yes, Lord," she told him, "I believe that you are the Christ, the Son of God, who was to come into the world."

"Lord, if you had been here, my brother would not have died." In that statement Martha gave voice to her doubt that Jesus had unlimited power. Had He been there, this would not have happened. He had to be present to heal her brother. Yet her general confidence in Jesus shines through: "But I know that even now God will give you whatever you ask."

Jesus answered her by turning her mind to the promise of the resurrection: "Your brother will rise again." Martha seemed impatient as she shot back, "Yes, Lord, I know he will rise again in the resurrection at the last day."

She knew the truth. She had the doctrine down right. In fact, she had a stronger spiritual base than the Sadducees who denied the resurrection. In her statement she bore witness to the strong teaching of her nation's faith. But she didn't find much comfort in the future tense. In that moment she needed something more immediate than an event as far off as the resurrection at the Last Day. The doctrine was not particularly consoling in her time of sorrow.

Jesus saw that and turned her idea of resurrection as a future event into a present reality: "I am the resurrection and the life." What must Martha have felt in that dramatic moment! "I am the resurrection and the life!" With those startling words Jesus brought Martha's thoughts from a dim future hope to a present fact. He gave her faith its true object, Himself. Confidence in Jesus Christ, the God-Man who is the resurrection and the life, could replace her vague hope in a future event.

How do we get that confidence? Jesus told us how in verse 25: "He who believes in me will live, even though he dies; and whoever lives and believes in me will never die."

When we believe in Jesus Christ, we gain a quality of life that is larger than death. Death becomes not the end of life, but the door into a larger life. People call our world "the land of the living." We might better call it "the land of the dying." We begin to die the moment we are born, and our lives are an inexorable move toward death. But those who have believed in Jesus Christ know that when death comes, we do not pass out of the land of the living but into the land of the living. We are not on our way to death. We are on our way to life. That's what it means to be born again. That's what it means to have eternal life. That's what it means to believe in Jesus Christ.

How did Jesus end His statement to Martha? He asked, "Do you believe this?" With that question He brought her to the question of personal faith. The faith that leads to eternal life can never be a faith we have inherited from our grandparents or that we acquire from being around the pastor. It is a personal commitment each one of us must make.

To Jesus' question Martha gave a remarkable answer (verse 27): "Yes, Lord, I believe that you are the Christ, the Son of God, who was to come into the world." Compare that to Peter's great confession (Matthew 16:16). Jesus had asked him, "Who do you say I am?" Peter had responded, "You are the Christ, the Son of the living God." Jesus responded that upon that confession, that truth, the church would be built.

Martha understood the same truth. Where had she learned it? Had she sat at Jesus' feet? Had she listened to Him teach the crowds? Clearly this woman, though her faith was imperfect, grasped the central truth on which it could grow: Jesus is the one sent by God.

It is the same for us today. It is on the truth Martha spoke that day in Bethany two thousand years ago that you and I come to the One who is the resurrection and the life. We cannot begin to grow until we see Jesus for who He is and we come to Him as we are.

The story moves on. Martha returned to the house and, taking Mary aside, told her that the Teacher had arrived and asked for her. Mary got up quickly and went to meet Jesus. She, in turn, spoke the same words Martha had used: "Lord, if you had been here, my brother would not have died." The same words Martha had used, but with one omission. Martha had gone on to say, "But I know that even now God will give you whatever you ask." Martha, for all her shortcomings, spoke of her faith. Mary, in contrast, was overwhelmed by her grief. She had sat at Jesus' feet and learned from Him. But now in His presence she was wrung out with her all-consuming sorrow.

When we read the other Mary-Martha story in Luke 10, it appeared that Mary was the "spiritual" one and Martha was the "unspiritual" one. Now as we look at these same two women, we discover that practical Martha had understood enough to give a magnificent confession of faith in Jesus Christ. Mary, on the other hand, was too engulfed in her loss to do more than say, "Jesus, if you had been here, my brother would not have died."

Note how Jesus adjusted to each one's need. With Martha, even in a time of deep mourning, He spoke deep theological truth. With Mary He sympathized. He met her where she was so that He could take her to a different level of faith. Thus it is with each of us. God starts with us where we are. But He doesn't leave us there. He moves us to a deeper level of faith.

The stage was now set. Four days had passed since Lazarus died. The usual Palestinian tomb was a cave with shelves cut in the rock on three sides. At the opening of the tomb a groove was made in the ground and a great wheel-shaped stone was set in the groove so it could be rolled across the entrance to the cave. For the Jews it was important that the entrance be well sealed. They believed that the spirits of the departed hovered around the tombs for four days, seeking entrance again into the body of the departed one. But after four days they left because by then the body would be so decayed they could no longer recognize it.

The mourners had followed Mary and now gathered in front of the cave. The oriental point of view was that the more unrestrained the mourning, the more honor they paid to the dead. These who had come to comfort Mary and Martha were not quietly weeping with heads averted. Instead, they honored Lazarus with unrestrained wailing, with hysterical shrieking.

Jesus stood in the midst of the crowd of mourners. In both verses 33 and 38 John described Him by using a Greek word that is not accurately translated in many Bibles. Jesus was more than "deeply moved." He shuddered with indignation.

Indignation at what? Jesus stood there that day as the Lord of Life, the one who had just told Martha that He was the resurrection and the life. There He was face to face with all the effects of the Fall: death, human misery, broken hearts. He had come into the world to deliver us from death and condemnation. He knew that as He confronted and conquered death that day, the final conquest could come in only one way. He, too, would have to pass through death. He would have to taste its bitterness. He would have to die.

He shuddered—shuddered at the awfulness of death. He shuddered at the consequences of sin. He shuddered at the pain of alienation. He shuddered with indignation that any of this had to happen. And then He acted. He spoke four times.

Speaking to the mourners, He simply said, "Take away the stone" (John 11:39). Jesus could have told the stone to roll away without human help, but He didn't. Those who stood there that day were given that task. God works with an economy of divine power. He requires us to do what we can do. He tests us by involving us in His miracles. "Take away the stone."

Had the Jews standing there heard correctly? Take away the stone? Surely Jesus couldn't be serious! Martha echoed their thoughts when she protested, "But, Lord! By this time there is a bad odor, for he has been there four days!" Martha just missed the point of that conversation out on the roadside. Jesus had to remind her, "Did I not tell you that if you believed, you would see the glory of God?" (verse 40). Jesus worked to raise Martha's faith to a higher level so that she could look beyond the earthly, the practical, and the mundane to see spiritual reality. "Take away the stone."

The second time Jesus spoke, it was to God: "Father, I thank you that you have heard me. I knew that you always hear me, but I said this for the benefit of the people standing here that they may believe that you sent me." Martha had said she believed that. But did the others? Did Mary? Did the disciples? Jesus laid His divine claim on the line. He did it to lead people to faith.

The third time Jesus spoke, He addressed Lazarus: "Lazarus, come out!" (verse 43). The dead man stumbled out, his hands and feet wrapped with strips of linen and a towel around his face. The crowd fell back, awestruck. Were their senses playing tricks on their minds? They had seen a dead corpse carried into that tomb four days earlier. It could not be true that Lazarus was alive again!

Jesus had not prayed, "Father, raise him from death!" Nor had He said, "In the name of the Father, come out." He had told Martha that He was the resurrection and the life. He acted on His own authority. He was the Lord of life. And Lazarus came out.

The fourth time Jesus spoke, it was again to the astonished audience: "Take off the grave clothes and let him go" (verse 44). The gasping bystanders needed to touch Lazarus and see for themselves that He was not a ghost.

Two things happened. First, many of the Jews who had come to visit Mary put their faith in Jesus (verse 45). That was the immediate result. Second, word of this incredible miracle soon reached the religious leaders in Jerusalem. They saw Jesus as a threat to their power. They met to seal His fate with a sentence of death.

A sentence of death? Yes, for Him. But a sentence of life for all of us who believe. He is the resurrection and the life. The one who believes in Him will live, even though that person dies. Whoever lives and believes in Him will never die. Do you believe this?

The old storytellers in many lands tell of a fabulous bird, sacred to the sun, called the phoenix. This huge bird, covered with an iridescent rainbow of gorgeous feathers, had no equal on earth. Not only was no other bird so beautiful, but none other sang so sweetly nor lived so long. The storytellers could not agree on the age of the phoenix. Some said the bird lived for five hundred years. Others said its life was more than twelve thousand years long.

When those years ended the phoenix made itself a nest of twigs from spice trees, set its nest on fire, and, with the nest, was consumed. Nothing remained except a scattering of ashes on the earth. But then, the storytellers said, a breeze caught those ashes and somehow from them there arose another phoenix, a new firebird even more splendid than the one that had died. He would spread his wings, they said, and he would fly up to the sun.

The storytellers spun this myth in the fond hope that somehow it could be true. They spoke to something deep within each of us, the longing that out of the destructive tragedies of life, something better, more magnificent might come. What the storytellers could only imagine contains a truth of which Jesus Christ is the reality. Just as the more glorious phoenix can rise only from the ashes of its dead self and ruined nest, so great faith rises only from our dashed hopes and ruined dreams.

"If God wants you to trust Him," wrote Donald Gray Barnhouse, "He puts you in a place of difficulty. If He wants you to trust Him greatly, He puts you in a place of impossibility. For when a thing is impossible, then we who are so prone to move things by the force of our own being can say, 'Lord, it has to be you. I am utterly, absolutely nothing.' "

Lazarus lived only to die again. A second time the sisters went to the tomb with the corpse of their beloved brother. This time there was no resurrection. But Jesus had taken Martha's theology and had given it vitality: "He who believes in me will live, even though he dies; and whoever lives and believes in me will never die." If you believe in a God of resurrection, you can face the cemetery and know that even out of death can come life. It is, in the words attributed to St. Francis of Assisi, in dying that we live.

But not all funerals lead to life. When Mae lost her only son, she lost sight of God and His power and love. She could not see that the phoenix rises from the ashes of its own death. She missed the reality that life invades death. She forgot—or never knew—that Jesus Christ passed through death to conquer it for all time and eternity.

As we experience the pain of loss, we can miss the phoenix. Yet Jesus speaks the same words to us that He spoke to Martha two thousand years ago on the road into Bethany: "I am the resurrection and the life." After death comes resurrection. We can trust God's perfect timing. We can trust His love. We can come through our difficult experiences stronger in faith and hope as we learn that God is there for us in our loss, in our sorrow. What we let Christ do in our situation makes the difference.

Questions for personal reflection or group discussion:

1. When you think of Martha and Mary, what do you think were stumbling blocks to faith for them?
2. Can you identify some stumbling blocks to faith in your life? If so, what are they?
3. How can knowing who Jesus is make a difference in your faith?
4. How can you experience immediate benefits (that is, power or strength) from your faith?

The *Canaanite Woman*: How to Pursue Faith in Life's Crises

Most of us who are parents have experienced those moments of inner panic that come when one of our children must be rushed unconscious to a hospital after an accident or when their temperature shoots to 105 degrees in the middle of the night. Though my children are now adults, I still get a knot in my stomach when I remember how helpless and desperate I felt each time that happened. In those moments we pray, not just in our heads but from somewhere in our guts, knowing that all the resources for saving our child lie outside ourselves.

If we get to a doctor in time, we may learn that an antibiotic or a hospital stay will be enough to return our child to health. Or the specialists may tell us that this priceless little child will live out her life with a disability. That can be a sentence of death-in-life that may send us on an endless search for a different diagnosis or a miracle cure.

Mark tells us of a desperate mother:

> As soon as she heard about [Jesus], a woman whose little daughter was possessed by an evil spirit came and fell at his feet. The woman was a Greek, born in Syrian Phoenicia. (7:25)

A demon-possessed daughter. What must that have meant for this frantic mother? Clinicians examining demon possession from New Testament times to our present day have found three characteristics almost always present in the demon-possessed person.

First, the facial features are distorted, sometimes so much that the person is no longer recognizable. Along with this, a demon-possessed person will in some cases contort his body or become physically agitated. Second, the voice changes, often deepening to the point that a woman's voice sounds like a man's. Third, the person displays a different personality. A normal person may become coarse and filthy. A gentle person may become aggressive and harsh. A refined person may use only gutter language.

Case histories underline the extraordinary strength of such people. In documented cases it has taken three or four adults to hold down a demon possessed child.

What terror this mother must have felt as she watched her little girl become someone unrecognizable to her. To see the sparkle in her eyes displaced by a glittering hardness. To see her smile twist into a sinister grimace. To hear a voice that was not her little girl's voice. To expect the familiar voice and hear deep bass tones and strange pronunciations. To watch a personality emerge that is alien and repulsive. Where had her little girl gone? What had happened to her daughter who could no longer be held and loved? What could be done to bring back the gentle child who had disappeared inside the body of this monster?

What had gone wrong? What could she have done to keep this from happening to her little girl? How had she failed as a mother? How could she appease the gods for her failure and thus free her daughter from this cursed demon?

What must it have been to live each day in fear, not knowing what it would bring? Would her child embarrass her? Attack her? Turn viciously on children in the neighborhood? Tormenting herself day and night, this desperate mother must have reached out for any possible remedy that could release her daughter from this bondage.

We don't know how the woman heard about Jesus. Nor do we know what she heard. What had someone told her that made her so sure He could help her? We know only that she had heard something that drove her to come to Him for help.

As our story opens, Jesus had been ministering in Galilee, the Jewish province in northern Palestine, beyond Samaria. For reasons not explained to us in the text, Jesus chose to withdraw from Jewish territory to a neighboring country on the Mediterranean coast:

> Jesus left that place [near the Sea of Galilee] and went to the vicinity of Tyre. He entered a house and did not want anyone to know it; yet he could not keep his presence secret. (Mark 7:24)

Even up in Galilee, several days' journey by foot from the Jewish capitol of Jerusalem, Jesus could not get away from the religious leaders who hounded Him wherever He went. Mark 7 opens with some Pharisees and teachers of the Law coming up from Jerusalem and attempting to trap Jesus into speaking against the Law of Moses. After a debate about what was ritually clean or unclean, Jesus turned away from the religious leaders and addressed the large crowd that followed Him wherever He went: "Listen to me, everyone, and understand this. Nothing outside a man can make him 'unclean' by going into him.

Rather it is what comes out of a man that makes him unclean" (7:14).

This was a sore point with the religious leaders throughout Jesus' earthly ministry. They had spent their lives keeping all the minutiae of the Law. They lived in dread of any contamination from the outside that would make them ritually unclean. When this young rabbi let His followers eat without obeying all the rituals of washing, it threatened all they believed. It challenged the profession they had given their lives to following. It could destroy their supporters' confidence in this legalistic way of life. In short, if Jesus continued to say these things, He could put them out of business.

It's not clear whether Jesus left the region around the Sea of Galilee because the confrontation with the religious leaders was leading prematurely to the cross He knew lay ahead. Or He may simply have needed a break from the constant crowds that dogged Him night and day. We find Him taking refuge near the city of Tyre, hoping that no one would know He was there. But as Mark tells us, in no time word about Him got out. And a Greek woman, born in Syrian Phoenicia, found out about Him and came to Him for help.

Matthew 15:21–25 begins the story this way:

> Leaving that place, Jesus withdrew to the region of Tyre and Sidon. A Canaanite woman from that vicinity came to him, crying out, "Lord, Son of David, have mercy on me! My daughter is suffering terribly from demon-possession."
>
> Jesus did not answer a word. So his disciples came to him and urged him, "Send her away, for she keeps crying out after us."

He answered, "I was sent only to the lost sheep of Israel." The woman came and knelt before him. "Lord, help me!" she said.

All Mark told us is that the woman begged Jesus to drive the demon out of her daughter. But Matthew paints a picture of our Lord Jesus Christ that shocks us. The first time the woman approached Him, He ignored her. The text says, "Jesus did not answer a word."

We don't like to think of Jesus being unresponsive to someone in need. We prefer a Savior who is always there for us, ready to hear our prayer. Yet it is clear in the text that Jesus simply ignored this distraught woman. Whatever she felt at that moment, she didn't give up.

We know that because the disciples were annoyed with her. She must have been so persistent, so unwilling to leave that they could stand her no longer. They appealed to Jesus to send her away because she kept pestering them.

It wasn't that they were unaccustomed to crowds. They had just come from Galilee where mobs of people thronged them wherever they turned. They had been running interference for Jesus for months now. They were used to doing it. But something about this woman got to them. They begged Jesus to send her away because she was driving them crazy.

In verse 24 Jesus answered the disciples in a way that seemed to have nothing to do with their request. He said simply, "I was sent only to the lost sheep of Israel." The woman, still standing there, must have heard His remark. She would have found cold comfort in it. Did He mean that only Israelites—Jews—could expect any help from Him?

The Canaanite Woman

She had already acknowledged that He was a Jew. In Matthew 15:22 we heard her address Him as "Lord, Son of David." We don't know from this how much she knew about the religion of the Jews, but she knew about the great king David and she understood that Jesus was in David's line. Did she know—had she heard—that here was the Messiah of the Jews? We don't know. But her way of addressing Jesus tells us that she knew something about who He was that made her persist in the face of silence, and then exclusion.

Nothing deterred her. In verse 25 we read, "The woman came and knelt before him. 'Lord, help me!' she said."

Then came a third kind of refusal. We find it in Mark 7:27: " 'First let the children eat all they want,' he told her, 'for it is not right to take the children's bread and toss it to their dogs.' "

Do Jesus' words seem even more harsh? No matter how we interpret this, Jesus appears to insult this foreign woman. Jesus called Gentiles "dogs" in the same way that people today may use pejorative names for people of other nationalities. To call someone a "dog" in first-century Palestine was insulting.

In the Middle East in Jesus' time a dog was never allowed indoors. Dogs were despised as filthy creatures. They roamed around, uncared for and half wild. A dog prowled through the streets searching for food. In temperament these wild dogs were not much different from wolves. Adult Middle Easterners would not associate with dogs.

In essence Jesus told this woman that the Jews needed to be fed first. What rightfully belonged to them should not be given away to others until their needs were met. But this bright, witty woman was not put off by Jesus' statement: "Yes, Lord," she replied, "but even the dogs under the table eat the children's crumbs" (Mark 7:28). She heard Him use a word for "dogs" that really meant "puppies." That was all she needed to hear.

In Middle Eastern families with children, little dogs—puppies—were allowed in the house as playthings for the children. Their place during mealtime was under the table. They caught the crumbs. And probably they also caught bits of food slipped under the table by sympathetic children.

She responded, "Yes, Lord, what you say is true. But even the puppies under the table eat the children's crumbs." Imagine Jesus with a twinkle in His eye and a playful tone in His voice. Something He did or said gave this woman hope and the courage to respond as she did.

Had Jesus said what He did in a harsh voice, she may have answered Him with bitterness. But His voice must have belied His words. She entered into the spirit of the test and responded to His words brilliantly: "Yes, the children must be fed. No one questions that. But puppies are still able to get the crumbs. The Jews have a full portion in you. They have your presence. They have your word. They sit at your feet. Surely they won't grudge me what I ask. Casting the demon out of my daughter is no more for you than dropping a crumb to a puppy. No one will be deprived if you do this for me. Lord, you have so much that even while the children are fed, the dogs may get the crumbs without depriving the children. There is enough for your children and still something for me."

How did Jesus answer her? Matthew tells us:

Then Jesus answered, "Woman, you have great

faith! Your request is granted." And her daughter was healed from that very hour (15:28).

The faith of this woman is stunning. She had very little going for her. There she stood, a Greek woman born in Syrian Phoenicia, a Canaanite. She probably had a religious heritage very different from the Jews. The Canaanite religion was polytheistic. That is, the people worshiped many gods. In earlier times followers of that religion offered human sacrifices. Jezebel, wife of the Old Testament king Ahab, came from the same region of Tyre. She forced the worship of the pagan god Baal on the Israelites. Canaanite religion was radically different from the Jewish worship of only one God, Jehovah. This Canaanite woman knew very little about true religion, and much of what she knew was wrong.

In spite of her lack of training in the Jewish religion, in spite of the fact that she could not have heard a great deal about Jesus, in spite of the fact that she may never have seen Him before this encounter, she believed that He could help her.

Within Judaism Jesus had met with resistance and unbelief on every side. But outside Israel, He met a pagan woman whose faith staggered Him. Her faith was greater than His closest followers had shown. "Woman, you have great faith!"

As He said that, did Jesus remember having just rebuked Peter with the words, "You of little faith—why did you doubt"? In the chapter immediately preceding the encounter with this Canaanite woman, Matthew recorded the incident of Jesus walking on the sea (Matthew 14:22–34). There we learn that the Savior had sent the disciples ahead to cross the lake while He dismissed the crowds and went up into the hills to pray.

A strong wind had come up, and the disciples were not able to make much headway rowing their fishing boat across the sea of Galilee that night. In the middle of the night as they fought against the storm, they saw Jesus walking on the water. They were terrified. Jesus tried to dispel their fear by identifying Himself and by telling them to take courage and not be afraid.

Then Peter—bold, brave, brash Peter—shouted out across the waves, "Lord, if it's you, tell me to come to you on the water." Jesus invited him to come, and Peter got out of the boat and started across the water to Jesus. Then he saw the wind, lost confidence, and started to sink into the water. He yelled out, "Lord, save me!" Jesus immediately reached out His hand and caught him. Verse 31 records Jesus' remark to Peter: "You of little faith—why did you doubt?"

Peter, the Jew, a man brought up in the synagogue, one who had already traveled all over Galilee and down to Judea with Jesus. Peter, someone who had heard Jesus teach and preach, had seen Him heal the sick, cast out demons, and raise the dead back to life. Peter, who had every reason to have strong faith, to him Jesus said, "Peter, you of little faith—why did you doubt?"

To the Canaanite woman—a pagan woman without the right religious teaching, who had never seen Jesus before, who knew next to nothing about God's promises to the Jews through the prophets—to this Canaanite woman Jesus said, "Woman, you have great faith!" Jesus found faith where He did not expect it.

This contrast turns things upside down. We assume that the person with the greatest knowledge of the Bible will be the strongest Christian, full of faith in times of trouble. We don't expect much at all from someone who hasn't been to church or Sunday school. But here we see faith strong and persistent in a woman with next to no spiritual training or background. In contrast, we see the great apostle, the one who served as foreman or leader of the twelve disciples, the great preacher at Pentecost, the one to whom Jesus delivered the commission, "Feed my sheep"—to Peter came the rebuke, "Why did you doubt?" God will overlook ignorance, but He will not overlook unbelief.

Little faith. Great faith. Peter was influenced by His surroundings. He did well as long as he ignored the wind and the waves and just kept moving toward Jesus. But his circumstances distracted him.

The woman, on the other hand, would not let any thing turn her from her goal. She brushed off the disciples, she ignored Jesus' silence and His remark about being sent only to the people of Israel. She simply refused to let her circumstances sidetrack her from her goal.

Little faith. Peter was in precisely the same amount of danger of drowning from the moment he got out of the boat until he crawled back in with Jesus' help. While Peter thought he was in a lot of danger out there on the lake, he was actually in no danger at all. Jesus was there. Weak faith, little faith, swings like a pendulum between great confidence and great fear. One moment Peter was walking on the water. The next moment he was going to drown. When Peter threw himself into the sea and started walking toward the Savior, he proved that Jesus was worth trusting. But his trust evaporated when he focused on his circumstances.

We may think, "Yes, I'm more like Peter than I am like

the Canaanite woman. My faith isn't much. It swings like a pendulum. One moment I'm walking on water. The next moment I'm neck-deep in water and headed down."

Take heart. A little bit of faith is still faith. A drop of water is water every bit as much as a reservoir of water. A spark is as much fire as a blaze. Little faith is still faith.

Even better, little faith can become great faith. The Peter we meet in his later letters could write:

> In this you greatly rejoice, though now for a little while you may have had to suffer grief in all kinds of trials. These have come so that your faith—of greater worth than gold, which perishes even though refined by fire—may be proved genuine and may result in praise, glory and honor when Jesus Christ is revealed. (1 Peter 1:6–7)

Jesus found this genuine faith in a woman who pleaded for her child. She wouldn't let go. She wouldn't give up. She hung on even when Jesus ignored her and spoke coolly to her. She simply wouldn't take "no" for an answer. Jesus was her only hope for her child. She saw light in the darkness. She hung on as if Jesus had given her a promise instead of a rebuff. Spurgeon observed that great faith can see the sun at midnight. Great faith can reap harvests in mid-winter. Great faith can find rivers in high places. Great faith is not dependent on sunlight. It sees what is invisible by any other light. Great faith hangs on to God.

Jesus delighted in this woman's vibrant faith. He looked at her faith the way a jeweler looks at a rare but unpolished stone. He tested her as a master jeweler buffets and grinds the impurities away from the face of the gem. By His silence and His rebuff He polished her until her faith sparkled. Jesus used her affliction to make her faith shine like a rare jewel.

This woman's crisis—a demon-possessed little daughter—brought her to Jesus Christ. Without that crisis, she might have lived and died and never have seen the Savior at all.

Crises can be God's device to move us to new ways of thinking about Him and to new levels of confidence in Him. Although we prefer good health, sickness can be good if it leads us to God. We prefer security, but difficulties serve us well when they bring us to Christ.

A nameless Canaanite woman, a foreigner, reminds us that in our crisis experiences, we can hang on and trust God because He is the only one who is trustworthy.

Questions for personal reflection or group discussion:

1. Why do you think the Canaanite woman had "great faith"? Where did it come from?
2. What was Peter's problem that Jesus rebuked him for having "little faith"?
3. How can you show that you are a woman of faith?
4. What will be some of the results in your life if you, too, have "great faith"?

The *Hemorrhaging Woman*: How to Find Jesus in Your Pain

When my friend Joann met her future husband and they lived out a storybook courtship, she anticipated that their Christian marriage would be "happily ever after." A decade later, the marriage exploded in her face. Her husband left her for another woman, and she began the long, painful task of bringing up two young boys alone. Financial problems dogged her. The frustrations of being both mother and father, homemaker and wage-earner drove her into depression and sapped all of her energy. Loneliness became her constant companion.

One of her greatest disappointments was the lack of support she felt from the family of God. The past twelve years have been marked by an unending struggle to pay the bills, rear her two sons (now teenagers) to Christian manhood, and rebuild the self-esteem that had been pulverized by the divorce.

Most of us have friends, like my friend Joann, who stagger under seemingly unbearable burdens, but who still hope that somehow Jesus Christ can make a difference in their lives. If we walk with Jesus through the Gospels, we see Him surrounded by such people. Matthew 9 opens with a group of men who were beside themselves to know what to do about a paralyzed friend. They had heard rumors about the young rabbi called Jesus. Could He do something for their friend? They hoisted the man up on his mat and brought him to Jesus.

Later in Matthew 9 a ruler of the synagogue pleaded with Jesus to do something about his little daughter who had just died. As Jesus left the ruler's house, two blind men followed Him, calling out, "Have mercy on us, Son of David!" As they left Jesus' presence, a demon-possessed man, unable to talk, was brought to Jesus. In a single chapter Matthew shows us the desperate needs of very different people who had one thing in common: they hoped that, in the midst of crushing despair, Jesus could make a difference in their lives.

Matthew spills over with the compassion of Jesus for suffering people. It ends with these words:

> Jesus went through all the towns and villages, teaching in their synagogues, preaching the good news of the kingdom and healing every disease and sickness. When he saw the crowds, he had compassion on them, because they were harassed and helpless, like sheep without a shepherd. Then he said to His disciples, "The harvest is plentiful, but the workers are few. Ask the Lord of the harvest, therefore, to send out workers into his harvest field" (9:35–38).

In the middle of chapter 9 we encounter another desperate person, a woman who had hemorrhaged for twelve long years. Her story reaches us not only through Matthew's gospel, but through Mark's and Luke's as well. We begin exploring this woman's suffering in Mark 5:24:

So Jesus went with [Jairus, the ruler of the synagogue.]
A large crowd followed and pressed around him. And a woman was there who had been subject to bleeding for twelve years. She had suffered a great deal under the care of many doctors and had spent all she had, yet instead of getting better she grew worse.

Twelve years! While we aren't positive what this bleeding was, it is usually assumed that it was a continuous menstrual period—for twelve long years. Even in today's world with modern medicine to help us, that would be exhausting and debilitating. As for any modern woman today, for her it would have meant being sapped of energy. It meant constant suffering and weakness. It may have meant depression. But in the time of Jesus, it was much, much worse.

To begin with, her bleeding made her a social outcast. The nature of her ailment in Israel was particularly degrading. From a Jewish perspective a woman could not suffer from any more terrible and humiliating disease than constant hemorrhaging. Women with flows of blood were ritually unclean, literally untouchable.

The Law laid this down in Leviticus 15:25–27:

When a woman has a discharge of blood for many days at a time other than her monthly period or has a discharge that continues beyond her period, she will be unclean as long as she has the discharge, just as in the days of her period. Any bed she lies on while her discharge continues will be unclean, as is her bed during her monthly period, and anything she sits on will be unclean, as during her period. Whoever touches them will be unclean; he must wash his clothes and bathe with water, and he will be unclean till evening.

Leviticus 15 concludes with these words spoken by God to Moses and Aaron: "You must keep the Israelites separate from things that make them unclean."

Can you imagine the implications of being "unclean" for twelve years? Most commentators believe that her husband would have divorced her. Others suggest that she would have been obliged to leave him. In any event, she could not maintain a normal relationship. She would be cut off from all good Jews, both male and female. Even to come in contact with a chair she had sat on or a bed she had lain on was to contaminate oneself. Such a person would have to wash his clothes and bathe with water—and still be considered unclean until evening.

That was one consequence for this first-century woman in Palestine. She was isolated from all community life, avoided, excluded. She could not go to the temple nor to the synagogue. She was shut off from the corporate worship of God. And no one could touch her, brush against her in a crowd, or come in contact with anything she had touched. She infected everything.

How could she shop in the street stalls for fruits or vegetables? She could touch nothing. If she brushed up against the shopkeeper, he was defiled. How could she walk about town without contacting anyone? Imagine the terrible exclusion and isolation she lived with for twelve long years! Unclean. Unclean.

Furthermore, in her day a woman with continuous bleeding was suspect. People assumed she was being punished by God for some secret sin. This tradition went well beyond the Law of Moses. She was probably excommunicated, divorced, ostracized, all on the basis of a false notion of her illness. It is unimaginable to be cut off from everything and everyone important to you— your family, your home, your church, your friends. Would you torment yourself, asking why this had happened to you? For what unknown sin was God punishing you? Can you picture yourself spending twelve years like that? What weary desolation she must have felt!

The second consequence we read in Mark 5:26:

> She had suffered a great deal under the care of many doctors and had spent all she had, yet instead of getting better she grew worse.

The Talmud sets out no fewer than eleven different cures for bleeding. Some were tonics and astringents. Others were superstitious notions. For example, one remedy was to carry the ashes of an ostrich egg in a linen bag in the summer and in a cotton bag in the winter. I don't know how available ostrich eggs were in Palestine at that time, but I am sure this woman found one, cremated it, and carried the ashes as the Talmud prescribed.

Another "cure" was to carry around a barleycorn that had been found in the dung or feces of a white she-ass. Can you imagine trying to find such a thing? It would be one thing to find a white female donkey. It would be something else to locate a barleycorn in the excrement of that beast.

It is probable that this poor woman had tried all

eleven cures in the Talmud and had seen other doctors who prescribed equally bizarre, often painful, possibly dangerous remedies. She tried everything and had gone to every available doctor, Mark tells us, but was worse instead of better.

We meet her in that huge crowd of people pressing around Jesus. Probably she should not have been there. What if someone bumped into her and became infected with her uncleanness? She must have been desperate for a cure—anything to leave behind this life of isolation and humiliation.

Mark continues the story in chapter 5:27:

> When she heard about Jesus, she came up behind him in the crowd and touched his cloak, because she thought, "If I just touch his clothes, I will be healed." Immediately her bleeding stopped and she felt in her body that she was freed from her suffering.

A miracle! Twelve long years of continuous bleeding, and in that moment when she touched Jesus' cloak she knew she was healed.

Some commentators quibble about the fact that this woman's faith was tainted with superstition. She thought that just touching Jesus' clothes would effect the healing. Whether there was an element of magic in her faith is not especially important. What matters is that she had enough faith to believe that Jesus could help her. Somehow she had confidence that the slightest contact with Him would heal her.

She heard that Jesus was in town. A flicker of hope stirred in her mind. Perhaps He could help her. No one else had. Could she find Him? She crouched against a wall, trying to make herself as inconspicuous as possible so no one would recognize her and order her away. Would Jesus pass this way? Was there a chance?

The sound of an approaching crowd reached her. See both hope and fear in her eyes. Anxiously she pressed against a doorway, hoping against all her fears that Jesus would come her way. Perhaps she talked to herself: "If I can only touch His clothes. Do I dare? I'll contaminate the Teacher if I do. It will make Him unclean. But I've heard that He touched lepers. They were unclean, like me, and He touched them and healed them. But maybe because I'm a woman, He wouldn't want to heal me. If He's a good Jew, He prays every morning, thanking God that He wasn't made a woman. Then, too, I've spent all I have on doctors and I don't have anything left to pay Him with. On the other hand, I've heard that He takes pity on the poor." She struggled to hang on to hope as waves of despair rolled over her.

In the midst of her turmoil, the crowd pushed and shoved around the corner. There in the midst of the pressing mob was the Teacher, Jesus, the one who might help her. Desperation and hope propelled her forward, away from the shelter of the wall and doorway. So many people! How could she possibly get through such a thick mass of people? So weak. So tired. So frail. Carefully, as unobtrusively as possible, she worked her way through the throng, afraid every moment someone who knew her would order her back. Fear pulled her back. Determination pushed her on.

Finally, coming up behind Jesus, she reached out and touched the blue and white tassel on the hem of His robe. Every good Jewish man wore four white tassels bound in blue thread on the four corners of His robe—one in front, one on each side and one in back. This was called the hem of the garment. She reached out tentatively, then with desperate determination, grasped that tassel. The word Mark uses in the Greek means "clutch." She didn't just brush her hand against the tassel. She clutched it. The Law said she should not touch, but in her desperation, she not only touched, she clutched the tassel. And in that moment all the weakness and sickness that had plagued her every day for twelve long years was gone. Into her body flowed an indescribable surge of health.

In that moment Jesus ignored her superstition and focused on her faith. Follow the story in Mark 5, beginning with verse 30:

> At once Jesus realized that power had gone out from him. He turned around in the crowd and asked, "Who touched my clothes?"
>
> "You see the people crowding against you," his disciples answered, "and yet you ask, 'Who touched me?'"
>
> But Jesus kept looking around to see who had done it. Then the woman, knowing what had happened to her, came and fell at his feet and, trembling with fear, told him the whole truth. He said to her, "Daughter, your faith has healed you. Go in peace and be freed from your suffering."

Luke 8:45–48 tells essentially the same story but adds a few details Mark omitted:

> "Who touched me?" Jesus asked.

When they all denied it, Peter said, "Master, the people are crowding and pressing against you."

But Jesus said, "Someone touched me; I know that power has gone out from me."

Then the woman, seeing that she could not go unnoticed, came trembling and fell at his feet. In the presence of all the people, she told why she had touched him and how she had been instantly healed. Then he said to her, "Daughter, your faith has healed you. Go in peace."

"Who touched me?" Jesus asked. You can under-stand why Peter and the other disciples were puzzled. No doubt a lot of people were touching the Master. But this was different. Jesus knew He had been touched in faith.

Do you think He really didn't know who had touched Him? It seems clear that He wanted to lift this woman's faith to a higher level. She had believed in the magical power of His clothes. He wanted her to know that she had exercised faith in Him and that her faith, not the hem of His robe, had healed her. And He wanted to do that in front of the crowd. Up to that moment she had been an outcast. Now she was set in front of that mob as an example of faith.

What would you have felt had you been in her place that day? In an instant she was healed. She could tell. She knew it had happened. But now as she crept away in the crowd, she heard Him ask, "Who touched me?" Would He find out that she had done it? Would He punish her for making Him unclean?

Finally, sure that she would be discovered, she came trembling with fear. After she told her story of twelve years of illness and isolation, then of her touch and healing, Jesus called her, "Daughter." This is the only place in the New Testament where Jesus called a woman "daughter."

Relationship! After twelve years of being cut off from all relationships, here is one who puts Himself in relationship to her. Whatever cringing unworthiness or inferiority she felt after twelve years of isolation from everyone else, in that moment He affirmed her as a person and called her into relationship with Himself.

For twelve years this woman had been lost in the crowds of life. She had become all but invisible except when others feared she would contaminate them. But when Jesus reached out to her, she could not remain lost in the crowd.

Do you ever feel lost in the crowd? Do you sometimes feel invisible, unwanted? When we reach out to Jesus in faith—perhaps with only a little bit of faith—it is enough. He will find us, lift us up, and call us "Daughter" as He puts us into relationship with Himself. Even more, once He puts us into that relationship to Himself, we have all of God's love and all of God's power at work on our behalf. It's not a question that one person uses up more of God's love and power and leaves less for other people. Not at all. God's love and power are infinite. There is enough for all of us.

Augustine said, in reading this story, "flesh presses, but faith touches." Jesus can always tell the difference. He knew which was simply the jostling of the crowd and which was the touch of faith. He could tell the difference in Palestine two thousand years ago. He can tell the difference today. He knows the touch of need and responds to us.

Did you notice what did not happen in this story?

We did not see the woman begging and pleading to be healed. She simply reached out in faith and touched the tassel of His robe—and she was healed. Jesus did not make her go through any kind of ritual. It was enough that she believed. The moment she took hold, healing came.

Jesus' public ministry lasted only a short three years. He had much to do and teach. But He always had time for individuals who needed Him. He saw Zacchaeus in the sycamore tree. He saw blind Bartimaeus at the gate to Jericho. He even saw the thief on an adjacent cross. He took time for a woman who had been bleeding for twelve long years. He asked nothing more of her than that she should believe He had the power to do for her what she could not do for herself.

It is the same for us today. Jesus asks only that we believe that He has the power to do for us what we cannot do for ourselves. It's the only way we can be in relationship to Him. Our faith may be imperfect. It may be weak. But when we come with whatever faith we have, He reaches out to us with healing. And we, too, will hear His word, "Go in peace."

The Greek text actually says, "Go into peace." Isn't that splendid? Move out of restlessness and into peace. Leave turmoil behind and move into peace. What a magnificent place to live—in peace. That was Jesus' legacy to His disciples just before His crucifixion: "Peace I leave with you; my peace I give you. I do not give to you as the world gives. Do not let your hearts be troubled and do not be afraid" (John 14:27).

That promise given two thousand years ago to a band of followers in an upper room at that last supper before Jesus died is a promise that comes down the centuries to you and me. Go into peace. It is Jesus' gift to each of us. It comes to us as we reach out in faith and touch Him. He knows the touch of faith. He always responds.

Questions for personal reflection or group discussion:

1. What do you think it takes to come to Jesus in your time of need?
2. Jesus ignored the woman's superstitiousness and responded to her faith. Can you count on Jesus to do the same for you? Explain.
3. The woman thought she was lost in the crowd, but Jesus singled her out. What does that mean for you today?
4. Jesus did not merely heal the woman of her hemorrhage. What else did He do for her? How does that apply to you today?

Two Widows: How to Give and Receive Graciously

A friend recently changed jobs and moved into a new office. He invited me to stop in the next time I was in the neighborhood. When I walked into his office, I was impressed. On the wall behind his desk are several framed photographs—one of my friend with Billy Graham, another signed to my friend by Garrison Keillor, a third autographed to him by a United States senator. I had no idea my friend had acquaintances in high places!

Suppose we were invited into the office of Jesus Christ. Whose pictures would we find on the wall behind His desk? Would we find a picture of Zacchaeus, the rich but despised tax collector? Or of a nameless sinful woman who lavished her love and thanks on Jesus by washing His feet with her tears and anointing them with perfumed oil? Perhaps. But we might also find the picture of two widows—one to whom Jesus showed grace, and the other who showed Him thanks.

Widows. What does that mean to us today? Even in modern Western societies, a widow seldom has an easy time of it. In most cases, when her husband dies, a widow's financial base is severely cut. If she is over sixty-five, she is eligible for some Social Security benefits. She can get basic medical care through Medicare. She can receive food stamps if she needs them. There are a few structures in place to help the single elderly who are poor.

It's not a lot, but it can make the difference between life and death.

If a widow today is under sixty-five, she can count on little help except food stamps. She probably works to support herself. In most cases, she likely doesn't earn enough to do more than meet her basic bills. Women, on the average, earn only two-thirds as much salary as men earn for the same level of work. Worse, most older women do not have the skills to work at anything other than entry-level jobs. Unless a widow's husband has left her with good insurance policies and with the house mortgage paid off, a nice savings account or a good investment program, her standard of living has probably dropped significantly since she became a widow. That's one of the facts of widowhood today. She may spend her final years in genteel poverty.

In Jesus' day a woman was, for the most part, even worse off. As a rule, she was in a position of total dependence on a man—her father, husband, son, brother, or brother-in-law. When a woman's husband died, she had only a few options. If she had a son, he took over the management of his father's estate and she could stay on in the household. If she was childless, she usually returned to her father's house—if he was still alive. Perhaps things could be arranged so that she would have the opportunity to marry again.

Another option was to ask that the Hebrew law of levirate marriage be applied. You may remember the conversation Jesus had with some Sadducees back in Mark 12:18–23, a passage that makes clear what levirate marriage was about:

> Then the Sadducees, who say there is no resurrection, came to him with a question.

"Teacher," they said, "Moses wrote for us that if a man's brother dies and leaves a wife but no children, the man must marry the widow and have children for his brother. Now there were seven brothers. The first one married and died without leaving any children. The second one married the widow, but he also died, leaving no child. It was the same with the third. In fact, none of the seven left any children. Last of all, the woman died too. At the resurrection whose wife will she be, since the seven were married to her?"

Interesting question! It gives us a good idea how levirate marriage worked in Jesus' time. A widow was at the mercy of the brothers of her dead husband. If there were no brothers, or if the brothers decided not to perform their duty to her, she could be completely without economic security, not to mention emotional support or social acceptance.

What was the purpose of levirate marriage? Breeding. The whole idea was to ensure that she bore a son in the name of her dead husband. If she were beyond child-bearing age, it was unlikely that anyone would bother with her. A widow without a son to care for her in her old age was completely without resources.

Jesus met such a woman at a city gate when He intercepted a funeral procession. Her story begins in Luke 7:11–12:

Soon afterward, Jesus went to a town called Nain, and his disciples and a large crowd went along with him. As he approached the town gate, a dead person was being carried out—the only son of his mother, and she was a widow. And a large crowd from the town was with her.

Jesus, surrounded by His disciples and a large crowd of people, approached the town of Nain at the moment a funeral procession came out the gate. They could hear the mourners before the procession came into view. Some of the townsfolk sang a lamentation. Others cried out, "Alas! Alas!" Still others moaned and beat their breasts. The noisy procession pushed through the town gate and moved toward the burial site.

Then Jesus spotted the four men carrying the corpse on a stretcher. It wasn't hard to tell, despite the cacophony of wailers, who was the bereaved. A lone woman, weeping, stumbled along, overcome by her grief.

Can you imagine a sadder funeral—that of the only son of a widow? Here was a mother left alone with her family line cut off. Her husband had died some time earlier. Now her only son was also gone. She had lost the two most significant people in her life. Even more, she may have lost her means for survival as well.

The text tells us that Jesus felt compassion for her. His heart went out to her. Then He added action to His compassion. Luke tells us:

> When the Lord saw her, his heart went out to her and he said, "Don't cry."
> Then he went up and touched the coffin, and those carrying it stood still. He said, "Young man, I say to you, get up." The dead man sat up and began to talk, and Jesus gave him back to his mother.
> They were all filled with awe and praised God.

"A great prophet has appeared among us," they said. "God has come to help his people." This news about Jesus spread throughout Judea and the surrounding country (7:13–17).

Jesus' first action touches us with His compassion, but it seemed like a futile thing to do. How could He tell her, "Don't cry"? The woman had just lost her only son! Was He insensitive to her loss? Or was He able to turn her grief into joy? Only His second action could make sense of His first action.

Once again Jesus violated rabbinic practices by voluntarily touching what was ritually unclean. He reached out and laid His hand on the stretcher. The mourners stopped their wailing in mid-sentence. The crowd fell back. Who was this rabbi who dared to touch the bier of the dead?

Did the Lord need to do that in order to work a miracle? Not necessarily. When Jesus stood in front of Lazarus' tomb, He merely commanded the dead man to come out. He could bring people back to life with only a word. But here at Nain's gate in front of a huge crowd, Jesus did the unthinkable. He made Himself ritually unclean by reaching out and touching the contaminating bier. In that action He underlined once again that it is not what happens on the outside that sullies us, but what goes on in our hearts.

Then Jesus spoke: "Young man, I say to you, get up!" Townspeople and mourners looked at each other. The man must be mad! Couldn't He see that the person was dead? Every eye was riveted on the stretcher. People gasped as the young man sat up. They were even more astonished when he began to talk. Was this possible?

Who ever heard of the dead coming back to life? Yet they had seen it with their own eyes.

Had you been standing by Nain's town gate that day, what would you have felt? Amazed? Scared? Speechless? Possibly all of these.

The Bible tells us that Jesus gave the young man back to his mother. The stunned pall bearers lowered the stretcher. Jesus may have reached out His hand to the youth and helped him step out onto the road. Her face still streaked with tears, the widow rushed to embrace her now-living son.

Jesus did this amazing miracle for one reason: His heart went out to this poor bereaved widow who had just lost her future, her only son.

Faith wasn't part of the package. Jesus had no conversation with the woman about believing in Him, about having to have faith in order to see God's miracle. Jesus knew that when a person is struggling under a heavy burden of grief, it is not the time for a theology lesson. It is a time for compassion. Jesus did what He could because His heart was touched with the woman's misery.

It is a great thing to know that Jesus is touched by our sadness and reaches out to comfort us, without our having to merit or earn anything. We may easily get the impression that the Christian life is some kind of trade-off: if we have a certain amount of faith, we can expect a certain amount of return from God. More faith—more things from God. A kind of pious bargaining. But that's where we get it all wrong.

What Jesus did for that widow at Nain's gate two thousand years ago was to give her His gift of sheer grace. She had done absolutely nothing to deserve that miracle. Yet Jesus reached out to her in her sorrow and gave her son back to her. He gave her back her future. He does the same for us today. By grace and nothing else He gives us a future and a hope.

* * *

How do we respond to God's grace when we have received it? Jesus made sure that His disciples did not miss one important way of responding to God. The time is many months later. The scene is the temple courtyard in Jerusalem.

Worshipers at the temple first entered the outer court, called the Court of the Gentiles. Jews then passed through the Gate Beautiful into the Court of the Women. Only Jewish men could enter the innermost court, the Court of Israel.

In the Court of the Women—accessible to all Jews—stood thirteen collection boxes. They were called the "trumpets" because they were shaped like the bell of that instrument. Each of these thirteen collection containers had a different purpose. One was for gifts to buy oil, another for corn, another for wine, and so forth, items needed for the daily sacrifices and for the general maintenance of the temple.

We don't know much about how Jesus worshiped or what He did when He went to church. But one thing is certain: He was interested in the offering. Mark tells us how Jesus spent some of His time in the temple:

Jesus sat down opposite the place where the offerings were put and watched the crowd putting their money into the temple treasury. Many rich people threw in large amounts. (Mark 12:41)

We may think that God's interest in what we do stops with how often we pray or read the Bible. Not so. Jesus is keenly interested in what we give to God's work as well. When we go to church, He is as aware of what we put in the offering plate as He is of the songs we sing and the prayers we pray.

When He preached the Sermon on the Mount, Jesus made clear that where we put our treasure tells people where our hearts are (Matthew 6:21). The attitude we have about money tests the reality we profess. What we give or hold back demonstrates what our priorities are. No wonder Jesus was interested in the offering that day in the temple courtyard.

As He sat there, what did He see? Mark wrote that many rich people threw in large amounts of money. From Matthew 6:2 we can even imagine donors approaching the collection boxes preceded by hired musicians blaring on trumpets to call attention to the gift. In the midst of these wealthy donors, Mark tells us, "A poor widow came and put in two very small copper coins, worth only a fraction of a penny" (Mark 12:42).

Seeing this, Jesus did and said something strange. He called His disciples over, pointed to the widow and said,

I tell you the truth, this poor widow has put more into the treasury than all the others. They all gave out of their wealth; but she, out of her poverty, put in everything—all she had to live on. (Mark 12:43–44)

That may sound a bit ridiculous to us. Of course, she hadn't put in more! In fact, it was impossible to put in anything at all and at the same time put in less. According to the system in her day, one could not give less than "two mites," the two small copper coins.

Jesus was not talking about actual amounts of money. He was talking about proportions. What matters to God is what we give in proportion to what we keep. It is easy to think that because I can't give as much as I'd like, I shouldn't bother giving my little bit to God. That is exactly the kind of thinking Jesus wanted to counteract.

Whatever we are able to give to God—whether it is money, time, or energy—is measured not by how much, but by how much in proportion to what we are able to give. As Jesus explained to His disciples, "She, out of her poverty, put in everything—all she had to live on." The poor widow that day had to choose between having something to eat or giving to God. She couldn't give half to God and keep half for a bit of bread. It was a question of giving all to God or keeping it for herself. She chose to give all to God. It was her wholehearted devotion that grabbed Jesus' attention that day.

She might have come to the temple courtyard that day wondering if she should make such a personal sacrifice. After all, what little she had to give would hardly buy a bit of lamp oil for the temple sacrifice. Intimidated by the magnitude of others' gifts, she might have hung back, watching as wealthy Jews, with trumpets blaring, poured their money into the collection boxes. Did it really matter to God whether or not she contributed two tiny copper coins?

Even worse, everyone knew that the teachers of the Law, the people who maintained the temple system, were corrupt. Then as now, widows were particularly vulnerable targets of unscrupulous religious leaders who sometimes took advantage of them. While sitting in the temple courtyard that day, Jesus had just warned His listeners:

> Watch out for the teachers of the law. They like to walk around in flowing robes and be greeted in the marketplaces, and have the most important seats in the synagogues and the places of honor at banquets. They devour widows' houses and for a show make lengthy prayers. Such men will be punished most severely (Mark 12:38)

What does it mean that religious leaders "devour widows' houses"? The Pharisees, we learn from the historian Josephus, prided themselves on being exact teachers of the Law. In Judaism a teacher of the Law could not take any pay for teaching others. He was supposed to have a trade or a profession by which to support himself, and he was required to teach without pay.

Many Pharisees, however, managed to persuade ordinary people—often widows—that the most significant thing they could do was to support a Pharisee in the manner to which he would like to become accustomed. It appears that women were particularly susceptible to this proposition. Many widows were known to have spent all they had to support a teacher of the Law. Pharisees took advantage of these women. They often extorted great sums of money for advising them, or they diverted entire estates away from the owners for their own use.

Jesus had seen this and recognized what could easily happen to such women. Sitting in the temple courtyard,

He had just warned about teachers of the Law who devour widows' houses when His attention was arrested by a poor widow approaching the offering boxes. Now as she paused, clutching the two tiny copper coins—all she had—did she think about the corrupt leaders who would spend these coins carelessly? Should she deny herself necessary food when she could do so little and when her gift might be diverted to crooked people?

As she extended her hand and dropped the two coins into one of the trumpets, she knew that, in spite of it all, she was giving to God. It was more important to her to show gratitude to God than to have food. She came to worship God with what she had, with what she could give. Her devotion to God was from her heart. She gave all she had.

In pointing out this poor widow in the temple courtyard, Jesus teaches us that God judges what we give by the quality of our giving, not by its quantity. The person He held up as a model of generosity is someone who gave less than a cent. What made it worth more than the vast wealth of others is that it was all that she had.

During our years in a central Wyoming pastorate, we frequently hired a short, stout grandmother to babysit our four children. To do this for us, Mrs. Knapp had to drive an unpredictable, old car into town some distance from the mesa where she and her husband lived in a tiny house. At one point they were able to have running water installed in the house, but they could never afford to put in a bathroom. Had I been Mrs. Knapp, I'm sure I would have saved all the babysitting money and butter-and-egg money for a real, inside bathroom.

What often brought me up short was that Mrs.

Knapp babysat, not for a bathroom, but to have something to give to God each Sunday. As I dropped a tithe check into the offering plate each Sunday, I knew Mrs. Knapp was dropping in much, much more. Most of us gave out of our abundance. She, out of her poverty, put in all that she had. Jesus never missed seeing her gift.

Often weary, never sure her car would run, burdened for her husband, Mrs. Knapp always showed up at our house with a smile. She was earning something to give to God. And she was enriched by that.

When you and I give, we are doing something Godlike. And when we give, we put meaning and purpose into all our getting. It is, as Jesus said, "more blessed to give than to receive" (Acts 20:35).

I stood in my friend's office admiring the pictures on his wall. And I thought of the pictures Jesus might have on His wall. Surely Mrs. Knapp's picture will be there, next to that of the widow in the temple courtyard.

By grace Jesus gave one widow her future. By grace Jesus Christ gives each of us a future and a hope. As we come to understand that, we begin to see why, like the widow in the temple courtyard, we can give to Jesus all that we have. Two tiny coins? We can part with them. Whatever we have, we can give to God freely and fully, not because we bargain with Him, but because we have received freely of His grace.

> We give Thee but Thine own,
> Whate'er that gift may be,
> All that we have is Thine alone,
> A trust, O Lord, from Thee.

Grace and giving. God's grace goes out to the helpless, and it is often from the helpless that the greatest praise comes to God. The more we understand God's grace, the more freely we give to God.

Questions for personal reflection or group discussion:

1. As you think about Jesus' compassion for the widow of Nain, what promise does that incident hold out to you as a follower of Jesus today?
2. How do you feel about receiving grace from the hand of God without being able to pay Him back?
3. What do you think Jesus meant when He said that the widow had put more into the temple treasury than all the rich people who had tossed in large amounts? How does that apply to what we can give God today?
4. Have you had experiences that show that God cares for helpless women today just as He cared for them two thousand years ago? If so, describe your experiences.

A *Sinful Woman*: How to Cultivate an Attitude of Gratitude

Gratitude can be a slippery thing to express. Some people have a way with words and sound wonderfully grateful even when they're not. The words, tone of voice, and gestures are all exactly right. But something puts us off: we detect the insincerity and we doubt that we are hearing genuine appreciation. Other people want desperately to express their gratitude but never seem to find the right words to communicate what they feel. They stumble over their tongue and then fall silent, afraid that if they say anything, it will come out wrong. Then there are the folks who never understand their indebtedness to a family member or a friend and make no effort to say thanks. Most of us have a hard time dealing with someone who takes another's kindnesses for granted.

The gospel writers recorded stories about Jesus' encounters with pairs of people who could not be more different in their attitude toward gratitude. We find one such pair in Luke 7. Simon is a punctilious Pharisee, the nameless woman a "sinner." He was outwardly civil but had no warmth. She broke conventions to express her love. He responded to the gift of forgiveness with a cool "Oh." She lavished her Lord with her gratitude.

Luke starts the story this way:

One of the Pharisees invited Jesus to have dinner

with him, so he went to the Pharisee's house and reclined at the table. When a woman who had lived a sinful life in that town learned that Jesus was eating at the Pharisee's house, she brought an alabaster jar of perfume, and as she stood behind him weeping, she began to wet his feet with her tears. Then she wiped them with her hair, kissed them and poured perfume on them. (7:36–38)

The scene is laid in Galilee. Jesus had just healed a centurion's servant who had been close to death. A day later He intercepted a funeral procession at Nain's city gate and restored a dead son to his widowed mother. The rumors flying across the countryside about this astonishing young rabbi from Nazareth seemed to become more unbelievable every day. A Pharisee named Simon knew it was time to arrange a meeting with Him.

If he gave a dinner party and included Jesus in the guest list, Simon could avoid having to mingle with townsfolk in the marketplace. It would also give Him an up-close opportunity to study this potentially-dangerous new teacher. The last time Jesus had preached in their synagogue and marketplace, some of the worst people in town had shown up. The gossip was that some of those people got "converted." In fact, the word was that a town prostitute had gotten the idea from the rabbi's preaching that even she could be forgiven by God and could be given a new beginning. Simon was sure that righteousness couldn't be bought with a mere prayer.

Jesus and His disciples arrived and the meal started. Then, unexpected and uninvited, a woman came in and stood behind Jesus weeping, wetting His feet with her tears, wiping His feet with her hair, then pouring perfume on them.

For most of us today that scene doesn't jibe with anything in our experience of modern houses, modern tables, modern chairs, or modern customs. Did people just wander into houses uninvited while people ate?

In first-century Palestine meals were often almost public. Spectators could crowd around as the guests dined. It was not unusual that an uninvited person should show up during the dinner party.

From Leonardo DaVinci's famous painting of the Last Supper we may have the impression that Jesus and His disciples sat on stools with their legs under the table, as we do today. That was not the case. Guests reclined on couches set like wheel spokes around the table. They leaned on their left side and reached for food with their right hand, the top part of their bodies toward the table and their feet stretched out behind them. Sandals had been removed at the door. It was easy enough for this woman to enter the house, stand behind Jesus and weep, only to have her tears fall on His extended feet.

Luke tells us that she was a woman who had led a sinful life. The words used to describe her are sometimes translated "prostitute" elsewhere in the New Testament. If not truly a prostitute, she may have been an abandoned woman. One commentator suggests that she may have passed her life in crime. Whatever she had done to merit her peculiar label, she was known in the community as a sinful woman. The startling thing was that such a woman would make her way to the house of Simon, a Pharisee, of all people.

Pharisees had a reputation for avoiding anything or anyone who might contaminate them. The word

Pharisee itself means "separation." During the four-hundred-year period between the end of the Old Testament and the beginning of the New Testament a group of men formed an order, called the Pharisees, committed to keeping the Jewish people from mixing with the idolatrous people around them. In the process they became satisfied with a religion that focused on externals like ritual washings and precise offerings. Certainly a sinful woman would not be welcome in their presence. It was unheard-of that a sinner should venture into the house of a Pharisee. What gave this woman the courage to appear in the house of Simon that day?

She dared come to Simon's house for only one reason: she had heard that Jesus was there. From the story Jesus later told Simon, it is certain that the woman had already received forgiveness for her many sins. She had possibly heard Jesus teach or preach and had become conscience-stricken because of her sinful life. Now that she knew where to find Him again, she had come.

She may have entered the door with some hesitation, but once she spotted where Jesus was reclining at the table, she passed quickly behind the other guests to His place. Tears blinded her as she bent over the feet of the Teacher. This was the one who had told her about God's forgiveness. This one had given her all she needed to start life again. Overcome by her gratitude, she could not hold back her tears. They spilled over the Teacher's feet. Reaching up and loosening her hair, she used it to begin wiping the Teacher's feet.

That act of unbinding her hair seems inconsequential to us today, but first-century Jewish women would never allow anyone outside their families to see them with loosened hair. Yet, oblivious to public opinion, this woman did the unthinkable: she let down her hair and used it to towel Jesus' feet dry.

Suspended around her neck on a cord was a perfume flask made of alabaster. These flasks were considered so much a part of a Jewish woman's dress that wearing them even on the Sabbath was not forbidden. To use the perfumed oil, the wearer broke off the long, thin neck of the flask and poured out the contents. As this woman dried her tears from Jesus' feet, she reached for the flask, snapped off the neck, and slowly anointed those feet with the perfumed oil. Suddenly the room was filled with the exquisite fragrance. If others had paid no attention to the woman to that point, they could ignore her actions no longer.

Love. Grateful love. Unconscious of the stares, the hisses, the rude comments, this woman poured out her love with that perfumed oil. She lavished that love on the one who had freed her to begin life anew.

When the Pharisee who had invited him saw this, he said to himself, "If this man were a prophet, he would know who is touching him and what kind of woman she is—that she is a sinner."

Jesus answered him, "Simon, I have something to tell you."

"Tell me, teacher," he said. (Luke 7:39–40)

Because Jesus had not drawn back from this woman and ordered her away, Simon inferred that the Teacher could not know her character. The Jews believed that being able to discern spirits was an important mark of the Messiah, the great prophet. When Jesus let the woman touch Him, Simon saw this as evidence that Jesus could not possibly be the Messiah. On the one hand, if Jesus didn't know what kind of woman she was, it proved that He was no prophet. On the other hand, if He did know what kind of woman she was and still let her touch Him, it would prove that He was not holy. Simon was sure that the Messiah would never deliberately choose to let a sinful woman make Him ritually unclean. Either way, it was clear that Jesus could not be the Christ of God.

Did Simon catch the irony of that moment? "If this man were a prophet, he would know." Immediately Jesus picked up on Simon's thought and responded to it: "Simon, I have something to tell you." Simon's answer was polite but cool: "Teacher, say it."

What followed was one of Jesus' marvelous little stories we call parables:

> Two men owed money to a certain moneylender. One owed him five hundred denarii, and the other fifty. Neither of them had the money to pay him back, so he canceled the debts of both. (Luke 7:41–42)

It was as if Jesus said to Simon, "It's true that one debtor owed ten times as much as the other, but both were debtors. Don't forget that, Simon. You may look down your nose at this woman because she has a reputation as a sinner. You surely don't think that you are not a sinner!" Of course, Simon would have answered that he was also a sinner, but not like that woman.

Some time later in His ministry, Jesus told another story about a Pharisee and a tax collector who both went up to the temple to pray. The Pharisee stood up and said, "God, I thank you that I am not like other men—

robbers, evildoers, adulterers—or even like this tax collector. I fast twice a week and give a tenth of all I get" (Luke 18:11–12). This Pharisee had no sense that he owed God anything. He may, if challenged, have acknowledged a small "five-denarii debt" to God. But to be placed in the same category of debtor like the tax collector or like a sinful woman? Never.

Drawing Simon into the story, Jesus then asked, "Now which of [these two debtors] will love the creditor more?" With grudging indifference Simon answered, "I suppose the one who had the bigger debt canceled." "You have judged correctly," Jesus affirmed.

Both debtors had nothing with which to pay their debt. Yet both were forgiven freely. Simon needed to see that although this woman had been a notorious sinner, she was forgiven. Her tribute of love proved her gratitude for God's forgiveness.

Turning toward the woman but still talking to Simon, Jesus asked:

Do you see this woman? I came into your house. You did not give me any water for my feet, but she wet my feet with her tears and wiped them with her hair. You did not give me a kiss, but this woman, from the time I entered, has not stopped kissing my feet. You did not put oil on my head, but she has poured perfume on my feet. (Luke 7:44–46)

"Do you see this woman, Simon?" Simon thought Jesus didn't see what sort of woman she was. Jesus knew that it was Simon who was blind. He could not see her as a forgiven woman. He could see her only as the sinful woman she had been. So Jesus set her in contrast to His host: "Simon, let me help you see her."

Jesus began by saying, "You didn't give me any water for my feet, but she wet my feet with her tears and wiped them with her hair." Simon bit his lip. It was true that he had deliberately ignored all the usual rites of hospitality toward his guest.

Jesus hadn't complained about Simon's cold welcome. But He had noticed it. Now He linked it to Simon's lack of gratitude for God's forgiveness. "Simon, didn't you just tell me that the person who has been forgiven a huge debt will feel great love for the one who forgave? This woman had a great debt. But it was forgiven. Now look at her gratitude! Look at her love! What does your treatment of me say about your gratitude?"

"Simon, you did not give me a kiss, but this woman, from the time I entered, has not stopped kissing my feet." The host normally greeted each guest with a kiss on the cheek. This woman, making up for Simon's deliberate coldness to his guest, gave the unusual sign of deep reverence for an honored teacher: she kissed his feet.

"Simon, you did not put oil on my head, but she has poured perfume on my feet." Once again Simon had ignored his duty as host by not anointing his guest with oil. Once again a grateful, forgiven woman did what the calculating Pharisee chose not to do.

In pouring perfumed oil on Jesus' feet, this woman performed a rite most often performed by men. Prophets anointed kings. Hosts anointed guests to refresh them. The disciples anointed the sick with oil as a cure. Women anointed only dead bodies for burial. This forgiven woman anointed Jesus, not on His head as Simon should have done, but on His feet—the body part assigned to slaves.

Jesus' last word to Simon before addressing the woman was, "He who has been forgiven little loves little." "Simon, do you get the point? You think you see so well, yet you see nothing clearly. You are religious—a Pharisee—and you draw back from this sinful woman. You thank God that you are not as this woman. You can hardly imagine entering heaven side by side with someone like her. But it is she who has experienced forgiveness. You haven't begun to understand forgiveness because you haven't begun to understand your need. I know you have been forgiven little because you show so little love."

Turning to the woman, Jesus said, "Your sins are forgiven." The perfect tense of the verb in Greek makes it clear that her forgiveness was not the result of her love. It was the other way around. She had already been forgiven. Here, in front of Simon and others crowding that dining room, Jesus publicly declared her to be a forgiven woman. Whatever she had been was past.

That forgiveness became the springboard for her lavish love. It is the same for us today. "We love [God] because he first loved us" (1 John 4:19). God starts the process by loving us unconditionally and forgiving us because of Jesus' sacrifice for our sins. The more we come to understand that forgiveness, the more we will love. Forgiveness is the cause. Love is the effect. Forgiveness is the reason and love is the result. Forgiveness is the root and love is the fruit.

Could Simon possibly understand what that sinful woman did that day at his dinner table? Did Simon give any thought to his own lovelessness? We love in proportion to our consciousness of having been forgiven. If we have no sense of debt to Christ, we will love little.

Jesus' last word to the woman was, "Your faith has saved you; go in peace." It was not her love that saved her. It was her faith. Because she was accepted by God, she could go in peace. She would probably never be accepted socially by Simon and his crowd. Others in the town might continue to look down on her. But they knew nothing of the grace of God. She could go in peace because her future was secure. She belonged to God.

In Luke's account our nameless woman was also wordless. The writer, in fact, gives us a conversation almost exclusively between Simon and Jesus about this woman. Only at the end does Jesus speak directly to her. Nothing is recorded that she might have said in response. Yet her deed spoke more eloquently than a thousand words.

At issue is not whether we can find beautiful words to frame our appreciation, but whether we feel the gratitude that impels us to find a way to express it. Do we understand, to borrow David's words, that God has brought us up out of a horrible pit, out of the miry clay, and has set our feet upon a rock and established our steps (Psalm 40:2)? Or do we feel closer to Simon, quite sure that God must be happy that such nice people as we have enlisted in His cause? As Jesus put it to Simon, "The one who has been forgiven little loves little."

When we see our sin and see God's grace at work in our lives, we will find a way to say thank you. It may be eloquently expressed in words. Or it may be even more eloquently framed without words as we give the best we have to the one who has saved us.

A Sinful Woman

Questions for personal reflection or group discussion:

1. What was wrong with Simon's attitude toward the sinful woman?
2. What was wrong with Simon's understanding of righteousness?
3. What do you think Jesus wanted Simon to learn from the parable about two debtors?
4. What do you believe it takes to be forgiven by God?

The Woman Taken in Adultery: How to Respond to the God of the Second Chance

When my office phone rang one day, I was surprised to hear the voice of a dear friend several thousand miles away: "Alice, I'm so embarrassed and humiliated, I don't know what to do. I've made a fool of myself over a man in our church. Here I am, a married woman, and I fell in love with this guy I've been working with in evangelism. It seems as if everyone in town knows how idiotic I've been. It has ruined my testimony at the church and it has mortified my husband. What should I do? Is there any way I can ever hold my head up again? Can God forgive me and give me another chance?"

I held the phone in my hand, and in that long moment between the time she spoke and I responded, I wondered how I should answer her. This was no academic question about forgiveness. It was the stuff of real life. When we've made a mess of things or have wasted our opportunities, can we start over again?

As I held the phone, I thought of another woman who had made a mess of her life. It nearly caused her death. Then Jesus came along.

* * *

Jesus was marching toward crucifixion on a Roman

cross. No matter what He did, the Jewish religious leaders determined to get Him at any cost. The "Get Jesus" committee was out in full force. If we glance back at John 7:1, we see that "Jesus went around in Galilee, purposely staying away from Judea because the Jews there were waiting to take his life."

It was autumn, the time of the annual Feast of the Tabernacles, one of the three principal Jewish festivals. Urged by his brothers to go with them down to Jerusalem for the feast, Jesus declined. But after they had left for Judea, He secretly made the trip to the capitol city for the feast.

In the midst of the festive revelry, it seemed that everyone was gossiping about the same subject: Jesus. Who was He? Some said He was a good man. Others thought He was a deceiver. Pilgrims, townsfolk, and priests alike asked the question, "Who is this man?" The seventh chapter of John rustles with mutterings, accusations, and conjectures about Him.

Again and again Jesus slipped through the fingers of the angry religious leaders. As the curtain goes up on chapter 8, Jesus was once more teaching in the temple courtyard. Those who hated Him most were making another attempt to trap Him. They had failed again and again, but this time it appeared that they had Jesus right where they wanted Him—caught on the horns of a dilemma. Follow the story in John 8, beginning with verse 2:

> At dawn [Jesus] appeared again in the temple courts, where all the people gathered around him, and he sat down to teach them. The teachers of the law and the Pharisees brought in a woman

caught in adultery. They made her stand before the group and said to Jesus, "Teacher, this woman was caught in the act of adultery. In the Law, Moses commanded us to stone such women. Now what do you say?" They were using this question as a trap, in order to have a basis for accusing him.

This "Get Jesus" committee had remembered the ancient Law of Moses in which anyone caught in the act of adultery should be put to death. That law had apparently not been enforced for generations. But the teachers of the Law and the Pharisees saw in that law the possibility of trapping the irritating rabbi from Nazareth.

To spring the trap they would need to catch someone in the midst of an adulterous act. In the Mardi Gras atmosphere of the festival that would not be difficult. The city streets were cluttered with hundreds of tiny booths, flimsy shelters of branches and leaves, constructed to last only the eight feast days. They had only to loiter on one of these streets and listen for the telltale sounds of lovemaking. Married people more likely made love in the privacy of their own homes. Finding a culprit should be simple.

They quickly rounded up a woman caught in the act. You may ask why they brought only the woman. Where was her male partner? The law stipulated that both should be stoned to death.

The context makes it clear that these religious leaders did not do this because they hated adultery. Nor did they do it because they loved godliness and wanted to uphold the Law. They simply hated Jesus. One guilty person would do quite nicely. They didn't need the man as well.

What was the snare in verse 6 that these leaders set

for Jesus? If Jesus said that the woman should be stoned, two things would happen. First, they could denounce Him to the Romans as one who usurped the prerogatives of the Roman government, the right to put criminals to death. Second, He would lose the love and devotion of the great mass of ordinary people who knew that His teachings included the need to show mercy.

On the other hand, if Jesus answered that she should not be stoned, they could say that He taught people to break the Law of Moses. Then He could be accused before the Sanhedrin as a false Messiah. Everyone knew that the Messiah must maintain or restore the sovereignty of the Law.

That was the dilemma they set before Jesus that day in the temple: infringe on the rights of the Roman government or deny the authority of the Mosaic Law. In their cunning they thought that, any way He moved, they had Him in checkmate.

There in the shadow of Herod's magnificent temple the drama began to unfold. Seated, perhaps in the Court of the Women, Jesus taught the crowds. Suddenly the sound of His voice was drowned out by scuffling feet and angry voices coming through the massive brass doors from the Court of the Gentiles. Approaching men jostled into the courtyard, dragging someone along. The crowd parted enough so that the scowling men could thrust a woman forward. People who had been listening intently to the Teacher now shifted restlessly, wondering what would happen next. They knew by the robes and headpieces that the intruders were Pharisees and teachers of the Law. And while some stared at the woman curiously, others looked away to avoid her shame as she stood there, disheveled, humiliated.

Then the religious leaders spoke: "Teacher, this woman was caught in the act of adultery. In the law, Moses commanded us to stone such women. Now what do you say?" Jesus didn't take them on in a debate. Instead, Jesus bent down and started to write on the ground with His finger.

No one moved. The terror-stricken woman looked into His face. What would the Teacher say? Would He condemn her to death? The tension grew as He said nothing. A few Pharisees glanced at one another with a glint of victory in their eyes. They had Him this time! He would know He was defeated.

Instead of speaking, He knelt on the ground. What did that mean? They repeated the question, "What do you have to say about this woman?" His finger traced Aramaic letters in the dust. They crowded closer to read what He wrote. By now the woman, still trembling, turned slightly to stare at the moving finger as the teachers of the Law pressed Him for an answer. At that Jesus stood up and made one comment: "If any of you is without sin, let Him be the first to throw a stone at her." And with that He stooped down again and continued writing in the sand on the pavement of the temple courtyard.

What He wrote is not recorded. Yet the word John used gives us a clue. The normal word in Greek meaning "to write" is *graphein,* but the word used here is *katagraphein.* That word can mean "to write down a record against someone." It may be that Jesus was confronting the teachers of the Law and the Pharisees with a record of their own sins.

"All right! Stone her! But let the man who is without sin be the first to cast a stone! You want your pound of flesh. You insist on keeping the Law scrupulously. Do what you think you must do. But only if you are blameless."

The word for "without sin" can also mean "without a sinful desire." Jesus was raising the bar. These legalistic religious leaders thought they had to jump only so high. Jesus said, "No, you have to jump this high. Not only your deeds count. Your thoughts and your desires count as well. Yes, you may stone her, but only if you never wanted to do the same thing yourselves." If they were going to be legalistic, they had to apply the same law to their own hearts.

Jesus moved the question from the legal domain—the Law of Moses—where the Pharisees had put it, to the moral ground of their own sinful desires. They operated on the basis of justice. Jesus operated on the basis of grace.

In Deuteronomy 17:6–7 Moses spelled out the procedure for stoning someone to death. There we read:

> On the testimony of two or three witnesses a man shall be put to death, but no one shall be put to death on the testimony of only one witness. The hands of the witnesses must be the first in putting him to death, and then the hands of all the people.

The death penalty was carried out by having one of the witnesses throw the accused from a scaffold, after which the other witness would throw the first stone or roll down a large boulder that would crush the accused to death. In doing this, the witnesses would feel the responsibility they bore in giving evidence. Any accuser in a capital offense had to serve as executioner. Jesus in essence said, "You profess to honor the Law of Moses. I remind you that this same Law requires the witnesses to be the executioners. Do you have clear consciences concerning the seventh commandment?"

Jesus knew the hearts of His opponents. He did not say that the woman had not sinned. Nor did He say that her sin should be shrugged off. She had sinned—against her husband and against God's law. But in the presence of her accusers, He did not mention her sin. He referred only to theirs. He reminded her accusers that they had no right to bring a charge against her. Their unchastity was notorious. Their own motives and lives were far from pure.

In that moment Jesus defended women for all time. In one sentence He laid down a single standard for faithfulness in marriage that applied to both men and women.

Verse 9 reveals what the scribes and Pharisees were really after. It was not to vindicate the purity of God's law. They simply wanted to get Jesus. If the Pharisees had been sincere in their indignation about this woman and her sin, they would have taken her to the officially constituted judge. But it was not her adultery they were against. It was Jesus. Seeing that their plan had failed, they took the only course remaining to them. They withdrew. In doing that, they silently admitted what had really brought them to the temple court that day.

What decided the matter was not that the woman hadn't sinned. She had. Jesus' point was that the motives of the witnesses were corrupt. Those who were to throw the first stone were technically qualified to do so, but they were not morally qualified. As Jesus sprang the trap on them that they had set for Him, conscience was at work. These men were wicked and hardened. Yet they felt something inside themselves they could not ignore. Supposed to be moral examples to the people, they knew their own hearts. Sheepishly, one by one, they slunk away.

Astonishment must have spread across the woman's face as Jesus straightened up and asked her,

> "Woman, where are they? Has no one condemned you?"
> "No one, sir," she said.
> "Then neither do I condemn you," Jesus declared. "Go now and leave your life of sin." (John 8:10–11)

Was it possible that her accusers had left? Could it be that her ordeal was over? Had she heard this Teacher correctly? Was He really saying that He did not condemn her? Was she free, really free to return home and start life over?

Some people, reading this account, have concluded that Jesus was soft on adultery. Others have accused Him of making a detour around the Law. Neither is true. We know from Deuteronomy 17 that no one could be accused or condemned except by the testimony of two witnesses. No one stayed to accuse her. With no accusers, the Law could say nothing.

Jesus neither condoned her adultery nor condemned her. He gave her another chance.

He did not treat the woman as if her sin didn't matter. Far from it. He did not say to her, "Your sins are forgiven." She had not repented nor had she asked for forgiveness. In saying, "I am not going to condemn you now—go and sin no more," He gave her a chance to repent and believe.

What she had done did matter. Broken laws and broken hearts always matter. But Jesus knew that every one of us has a future as well as a past. He offered this woman a second chance.

Jesus did not say to her, "It's okay. Go on doing what you've been doing." No. He said, "Stop what you've been doing. Go and sin no more!" He pointed her in a direction she might not have realized was possible.

Many times we continue to do things we don't feel good about because we don't know we have any alternatives. God says to us, "You have alternatives." Jesus gave her a choice that day. She could go back to her old life or she could reach out for a new life of purity under God's law.

The meaning of repentance is "to forsake sin." It means to change our mind in order to change our life. Repentance isn't just feeling sorry or saying we're sorry or wishing or hoping that we won't do something bad again. The life of repentance is action. Until we turn from what is wrong, we haven't repented.

Turning from the woman, Jesus addressed the crowd: "I am the light of the world. Whoever follows me will never walk in darkness, but will have the light of life." Did the woman hear His words? He called her out of darkness to live in the light. He had exposed sin in the religious leaders. He did not gloss over sin in this woman's past. He called her to walk in the light.

From the biblical record in John 8, this woman's story is unfinished. Jesus Christ, standing in that temple courtyard two thousand years ago, gave her a second chance. The Bible doesn't tell us what she did with that opportunity.

A more important question is what we do with the second chance, the third chance, the tenth chance, the hundredth chance that God gives us to trust Him, to follow Him, to serve Him. The story of our lives isn't over.

We may look back on a secret sorrow or on a blatant sin and think there is no second chance. That's not so. God reaches out to us with another chance.

Yet if we have spent more time listening to modern-day "teachers of the Law and Pharisees" than we have to Jesus Christ, we may find that hard to believe.

We all know religious people who live by the Law, who criticize and condemn us. They stand over us, watching for every mistake. They may descend on every misstep we take with savage punishment. Such people use authority to destroy others, not to redeem them, heal them, or cure them. They may be blind to the fact that "there, but for the grace of God, go I."

If you grew up with people like that, you may think that God doesn't give second chances or third chances to people who sin. Jesus has a different word for you: "I do not condemn you. Go now and leave your life of sin."

That is what matters. Not what is past but what lies ahead. Every day God gives us another chance, a new opportunity to follow Him, to serve Him, to love Him, to carry out His will for our lives.

I held the phone in my hand and thought of this woman who had mishandled life as my friend had mishandled hers. What did I know from Jesus' actions that would answer my friend's question: when you've made a mess of things, can you start over again? After a long moment, I spoke, "I can promise you this. There is forgiveness, full and complete, from the Christ of the second chance. Can you start over again? God's answer is 'YES, YES, a thousand times YES.' "

Questions for personal reflection or group discussion:

1. What do you imagine God thinks and feels about you if you have made a mess of your life?
2. Do you think some sins are harder than others for God to forgive? If so, what are examples of "big ones"?
3. How do you feel about God giving people a second chance when they've committed a grievous sin?
4. What do you think "grace" means?

Mary of Bethany: How to Make Jesus Your Priority

In *Beloved,* Toni Morrison's Pulitzer Prize-winning novel about Civil War-era Black slave women, Grandmother Baby Suggs decided to celebrate her daughter-in-law's escape from slavery. She invited friends and neighbors for dinner. In the end, ninety people came and feasted on turkey, catfish, and fresh berry pies far into the night. As the house rocked with laughter, someone raised the question, "Where does she get it all, Baby Suggs? Why is she and hers always the center of things? How come she always knows exactly what to do and when?"

As guests passed the question from one to another,

it made them furious. They swallowed baking soda the morning after to calm the stomach violence caused by the bounty, the reckless generosity on display at house #124. Whispered to each other in the yards about fat rats, doom and uncalled-for pride. The scent of this disapproval lay heavy in the air.

Baby Suggs, hoeing her garden the next day, tried to understand what was happening. "Then she knew. Her friends and neighbors were angry at her because she had overstepped, given too much, offended them by excess."

In the years that followed, she, her daughter-in-law, and her grandchildren faced one tragedy after another without the support of their friends and neighbors.

Baby Suggs' experience of rejection for her bounty reminded me of another woman who gave her best in one lavish gesture. She, too, was misunderstood and condemned. The woman is Mary, the younger sister of Martha and Lazarus. John tells her story this way:

> Six days before the Passover, Jesus arrived at Bethany, where Lazarus lived, whom Jesus had raised from the dead. Here a dinner was given in Jesus' honor. Martha served, while Lazarus was among those reclining at the table with him. Then Mary took about a pint of pure nard, an expensive perfume; she poured it on Jesus' feet and wiped his feet with her hair. And the house was filled with the fragrance of the perfume. (12:1–3)

Of no other person in the Gospels is it written that "wherever the gospel is preached throughout the world, what she has done will also be told, in memory of her" (Mark 14:9). What was so remarkable about Mary's act that Jesus would make such a statement? Her story merits a closer look.

Word had reached friends of Jesus in Bethany that He was returning to Jerusalem to celebrate the Passover. Simon, a leper whom Jesus had most likely healed, hosted a dinner party for the Lord. Martha—another good friend—served, and Lazarus, her brother, reclined at the table with Jesus and the other guests.

When Simon decided to organize a feast to honor Jesus, he took a great risk. In the verses immediately preceding Mary's story, John tells us that from the moment Jesus had brought Lazarus back to life, the chief priests and the Pharisees "plotted to take [Jesus'] life." The threat to His life was so real that

> Jesus no longer moved about publicly among the Jews. Instead he withdrew to a region near the desert, to a village called Ephraim, where he stayed with his disciples. . . . But the chief priests and Pharisees had given orders that if anyone found out where Jesus was, he should report it so that they might arrest him. (John 11:54, 57)

Not only did Simon take a risk inviting Jesus; he added to the danger by including Lazarus in the guest list as well. John reported that "the chief priests made plans to kill Lazarus as well, for on account of him many of the Jews were going over to Jesus and putting their faith in him" (John 12:10–11). Simon's gratitude to Jesus gave him courage to do what could get him into serious trouble with the religious leaders.

The dinner party was underway. In the midst of the festivities, Mary took an alabaster flask of very expensive oil of spikenard, broke the flask, and poured out the contents, first on Jesus' head, then on His feet.

One day, as I stood in line at the check-out counter of a second-hand thrift store, I noticed a full two-ounce bottle of cologne on a nearby shelf. With nothing better to do while waiting my turn, I pulled off the cap and sniffed the fragrance. It was enchanting! I had never heard of the Swiss perfumerie, but the price was right ($1.41!), so I added it to my other purchases. During the next year I used the cologne freely. Then the bottle was empty.

Some close French friends, planning a trip to America last year, wrote and asked what they could bring over for us. I dashed off a letter asking for another bottle of this exquisite but unknown perfume. To my delight, they brought me a bottle as a gift. To my astonishment, I learned that the two ounces of cologne I had used carelessly cost $75. Had I known its true value, I would have used it more cautiously.

Mary did not pick up her alabaster flask of oil of spikenard at a second-hand thrift shop for $1.41. She knew the value of her gift as she twisted off the top of the flask and began anointing Jesus.

One pound of oil of nard. Nard, squeezed from a plant grown in India, was the most expensive perfume in the world. Mark makes a point of telling us that Mary's nard was "pure"—not nard plus something else, and not an imitation. This was not cologne or eau de toilette. It wasn't a cheap copy-cat version of nard. No "If you like Giorgio, you'll *love* Primo!" It was the real thing, exquisite and extraordinarily expensive. And she had a "pound" of it, twelve ounces in today's measurements. One and a half cups. Do you know what she did with it?

Twisting the neck on the alabaster jar, Mary felt the thin, pastel stone give way. The delicious fragrance of the nard rushed up to her, and she smiled with delight. She lifted the vase up and tilted it slightly so that the perfume drizzled onto Jesus' head. It was a Jewish custom to anoint the head for feast days, and Jesus had come for the Passover Feast.

What Mary did was generous and she could have stopped there. But she didn't. Next, John tells us, she poured the fragrant oil on Jesus' feet. Just as if it were common water. She poured out so much nard that as it ran down His ankles and between His toes, she was obliged to loosen her hair and use it to towel off the excess.

Mary had sat at Jesus' feet (Luke 10:38–42) and had known His comfort and then His miracle when Lazarus, her brother, had died (John 11:28–44). Now, out of her gratitude and love, she responded to Jesus with the best she could give. She had already given Him her heart. Now she poured out the most costly gift she could offer to the one who had done so much for her.

The fragrance filled the room. No one present could ignore what she had done. She may not have heard the guests' gasps of surprise, but she could not miss the voice of Judas Iscariot as his cutting question sliced into her consciousness. "Why this waste of perfume? It could have been sold for more than a year's wages and the money given to the poor."

The sting of criticism. It's a lash we've all felt. What seemed like such a good idea to us looks stupid or thoughtless or selfish to someone else. The reaction takes us by surprise when that happens. We draw back from the cutting words. We expect people inhaling the fragrance to be pleased by it. Instead we are attacked. We ask questions we can't easily answer: Why are they frowning instead of smiling? Why is there more criticism than praise? What prompted this indignation in the place of approval?

Judas, with narrowed eyes, spat out his scornful criticism of this woman. He saw nothing good in Mary's act. At best it was extravagant. At worst it was evil. Think of the hungry who could have been fed. Think of the naked who could have been clothed.

What Judas said was accurate. The perfume could

have been sold and the money given to the poor. The alabaster flask had contained pure nard, worth more than a year's wages. (Calculating Judas knew the exact worth of her gift.) A year's wages would meet the needs of a destitute family for twelve months or more. A year's wages could finance a soup kitchen and feed many people. A year's wages could provide shelter for street children. Had Mary made a grievous mistake in pouring out her twelve ounces of nard in one lavish gesture of love for Jesus Christ? She must have wondered if she would have been wiser to do as Judas suggested. It hadn't even crossed her mind! Had she missed the point of Jesus' life and ministry to such a degree that she had wasted an opportunity to help the poor? She burned with embarrassment as she thought of Judas's condemnation.

As Mary stood there that day, empty flask in hand, staring in an agony of self-doubt at her accuser, she heard another voice respond to Judas.

"Leave her alone," said Jesus. "Why are you bothering her? She has done a beautiful thing to me. The poor you will always have with you, and you can help them any time you want. But you will not always have me. She did what she could. She poured perfume on my body beforehand to prepare for my burial. I tell you the truth, wherever the gospel is preached throughout the world, what she has done will also be told, in memory of her." (Mark 14:6–9)

What is the purpose of perfume, if not to be used to bring fragrance into someone's life? Is it merely a commodity to be sold to one buyer and then another, always changing hands in exchange for money, never being used? What gives it its value? Jesus told Judas that Mary had used the perfume in the right way: she had anointed His body beforehand for His burial.

Judas had heard Jesus' predictions of His impending arrest and crucifixion. He may have already concluded that Jesus was a loser. Only a few days later he would go to the chief priests and betray his Master for thirty pieces of silver. Judas placed Jesus' value at a handful of silver coins and complained that Mary set His value above a year's wages.

Judas sounded so sensible! By his criticism he placed himself on the side of the hurting and oppressed. But Jesus wasn't taken in by Judas's "concern for the poor." "If you really are concerned about the poor," He replied, "you'll always find opportunities to be liberal toward them. But Mary is doing something practical, too. In a few days when I am put to death, she won't have an opportunity to anoint my dead body. She's doing that now." Simon's dinner party was the scene of Jesus' funeral anointing.

When Jesus called Mary's deed "a beautiful thing," was He merely being chivalrous? Did she deserve such high praise? In Bethlehem a thousand years earlier as Samuel inspected each of Jesse's sons to see which one he should anoint as the next king of Israel, he was sure Eliab would be God's choice. But the Lord said to Samuel,

"Do not consider his appearance or his height, for I have rejected him. The LORD does not look at the things man looks at. Man look at the outward appearance, but the LORD looks at the heart." (1 Samuel 16:7)

As Jesus reclined at Simon's table that day, He looked beyond Mary's deed to Mary's heart. He had also looked beyond Judas's words to Judas's heart. Judas's criticism was ugly because it came from an ugly motive. Mary's deed was beautiful because it came out of her love for Jesus Christ. The worth or worthlessness of any gift depends on our motive. What we give to Jesus Christ for self-serving reasons will come to nothing. But what we give to Him out of love will never be forgotten.

Nothing, absolutely nothing that we do out of love and loyalty to Jesus Christ fails to be beautiful, no matter how silly or wasteful it may seem to others. God judges our deeds by the motives that prompt them. The smallest work done by the weakest woman will not be overlooked by God. In God's book of everlasting remembrance not a single kind word or deed, not a cup of cold water given in His name will be omitted.

Far from being wasteful and wicked, Mary had done a beautiful thing. She had given her very best. Jesus said to her in essence, "Mary, your deed is so beautiful, I will never forget it or allow the world to forget it. Hand in hand you will walk across the centuries with me. Wherever My story is told, yours will be told also."

Jesus gave great praise to women who were great givers. When the poverty-stricken widow approached the offering boxes in the temple with only two tiny mites between her and starvation, with reckless abandon she gave all that she had to God. He remarked to His disciples sitting nearby, "This poor widow has put more into the treasury than all the others. They all gave out of their wealth; but she, out of her poverty, put in everything—all she had to live on" (Mark 12:43–44). It was not a question of how much she gave but of how fully she gave.

When Mary poured more than a year's wages on Jesus' head and feet in one great gesture of love, Jesus approved of her gift. It is interesting that Jesus never had a word of praise for prudent, conservative giving, but He showed great enthusiasm for those who gave with abandon.

The honor roll of women who gave with abandon has continued down the centuries. Amy Carmichael turned her back on a secure and happy life in England to rescue young girls from temple prostitution in India. Mary Slessor left Scotland to plant churches and start schools in Nigerian jungles where no other European dared go. Three medical doctors—Maybel Bruce, Mary Wilder, and Ann Irish—gave up comfort and security in America to start a medical center for Muslim women in the hottest, driest, most draining part of Pakistan. Each of these women poured out the perfume of their lives in abandoned giving to Jesus Christ.

Mary's gift looked extravagant and wasteful. Judas said it did no good. But Judas had no scales for weighing what God values. To him the most priceless things seemed worthless. But Jesus put a different value on her gift. As she poured out her perfume with abandon on Him, He would soon pour out His life with abandon for her.

Bob Jones, Jr., captured this truth when he wrote,

A broken vase of priceless worth rich fragrance
    shed
In ointment poured in worship on Thy head.

A lovely thing all shattered thus—"What waste,"
   they thought,
But Mary's deed of love Thy blessing brought.
A broken form upon the cross and souls set free.
Thy anguish there has paid the penalty
Sin's awful price in riven flesh and pain and
   blood—
Redemption's cost, the broken Lamb of God.

We who serve the lavish God of heaven ask, "How can I repay the LORD for all his goodness to me?" (Psalm 116:12). We know that one of His blessings is to allow us in worship to pour out the best we have for Him.

Questions for personal reflection or group discussion:

1. Think of one experience in your life in which you gave Jesus Christ a sacrificial gift of your time, of your energy, or of your money. Describe that event.
2. As you think about that event, what did you get out of it? Misunderstanding? Appreciation? Criticism? Praise?
3. If you had it to do over, would you do it again? Explain.
4. Why do you think our motives are so important to God? Why shouldn't the deed be enough regardless of our motives?

Mary Magdalene: How to Walk by Faith and Not by Sight

In *Women's Ways of Knowing,* an important study of the way women think about themselves and about life, Mary Belenke and her fellow researchers identified five ways women know things. One of them is called "received knowledge." We all know things because someone told them to us. Most of us have a large fund of received knowledge, a stash of facts and opinions we didn't think up on our own but we accept. We "know" how to use a washing machine and grow houseplants, and where to buy the freshest vegetables or find the best book bargains. We may also have learned to name some of the constellations and all the books of the Bible. We've spent our lives acquiring this kind of knowledge.

Surprisingly, many women limit what they "know" to what they have received from someone else. They look to an authority outside themselves for instruction in every area of life. An interior decorator tells them which home furnishings to buy. A hair stylist decides how they should wear their hair. A personal shopper chooses their clothes after a color analyst has given them a swatch chart of colors to wear. These women know a great deal and know that they know a lot. But they trust only what comes from outside themselves as "real" knowledge.

Sometimes such a woman faces a crisis. Perhaps an authority falls from grace or disappoints her. Or two equal authorities disagree. Whom can she believe? At that point a woman may move to a different way of thinking about herself and about her world.

These studies about the way women think intrigue me. In most cases, it takes some kind of crisis, a confrontation, a disappointment, or a disaster to move a woman from unquestioning reliance on outside human authorities to a different way of thinking and knowing. She has to make room for new learning.

We seldom move from one comfortable level of learning and knowing to another unless we are forced in some way to move. I benefited most from teachers who made me think instead of letting me parrot the textbook or my lecture notes.

We don't do ourselves a favor if we insist on staying at one learning level when we need to move to another one. We often don't like the circumstances that push us to change. We'd prefer to be left alone in our comfortable tranquility. But that is not the path to growth.

Nor is it the path to true discipleship. If we are to grow as Christian women in our understanding of God, we have to expect the tough circumstances that confront and disappoint us. It takes grim life experiences to build muscle into our souls.

The process of following Jesus as His disciples is the process of making room for new ways of looking at life and at ourselves. In this book we have watched Jesus move His mother, Mary, to a different way of seeing her relationship to her Son. We have seen Him move Martha to a different way of viewing her service to God. We have listened in as Jesus gave a Samaritan woman her first drink of living water as she saw herself with masks stripped away. We have observed Him guiding two sisters to a different way of thinking about death.

Jesus was a master teacher. We might have expected Him to use only one method for getting His message across, but He taught different people in different ways. We might have thought He would choose only the most promising pupils for His class. Instead, He included men and women other teachers would have ignored. One choice pupil of the Master Teacher was Mary Magdalene. She possibly spent more time with Jesus than any other woman in the gospels.

Mary of Magdala found that her discipleship as a follower of Jesus Christ was a constant learning process. She had already learned much as one who traveled with Jesus. But in one of the final scenes in the Gospels, she was once again back in school, learning something new about being a disciple.

Though she is mentioned by name fourteen times in the gospels, we actually know only four things about Mary Magdalene. The first two we see in Luke 8:1–3:

> Jesus traveled about from one town and village to another, proclaiming the good news of the kingdom of God. The Twelve were with him, and also some women who had been cured of evil spirits and diseases: Mary (called Magdalene) from whom seven demons had come out; Joanna the wife of Cuza, the manager of Herod's household; Susanna; and many others. These women were helping to support them out of their own means.

The first fact we know about Mary of Magdala is that Jesus cast seven devils out of her. We don't know when or where. Both Mark and Luke give us the fact, but neither gives us the story. We do know from her name that Mary came from Magdala, a town about three miles from Capernaum on the northwest shore of the Sea of Galilee. It was the territory that Jesus continually criss-crossed in His itinerant ministry in Galilee. At some point they met and the miracle of her deliverance took place. Delivered from being possessed by seven devils. What must that have meant for this woman? We do not know how long or in what way she was tormented by demon-possession. But we do know that any possessed person was an outcast from normal society. Some afflicted people were more animal than human, living in caves, roving around the countryside terrifying people with their distorted faces and wild eyes. Created by God, they were being destroyed by Satan. What it meant for Mary to be possessed by seven demons we cannot guess. But for her, deliverance must have been a life-changing liberation. Her bound spirit was set free. Her cramped limbs relaxed. Her contorted face became serene.

The second thing we know about Mary is that she traveled all over Galilee and down into Judea with Jesus and the Twelve. If you suffered from a terrible affliction for years and then found a doctor who could release you from your suffering, you would probably want to stay as close to that doctor as possible. Mary Magdalene became a permanent itinerant with Jesus' band of followers.

Most of us probably assumed that Jesus and His disciples traveled around strictly as a male group: the Savior and the twelve men whose names we may have memorized in Sunday school. There are a number of reasons we might assume that.

For one, during the first century in Palestine, some rabbis taught that good religious men did not speak to women in public. A Pharisee would not speak even to his own mother if he met her on the street. The careful segregation of men and women in that culture would make anyone traveling with both male and female followers too counter-culture to be listened to.

Furthermore, the Law declared that a woman during her menstrual period was ritually unclean. Everything she touched was defiled. At such a time she needed to be tucked away where she could not contaminate anyone else. How could Jesus and the Twelve risk contamination by these women traveling with them?

Public opinion about a mixed band of followers traveling around with Jesus might have raised moral questions. When we think about Jesus and His disciples in the Gospels, the people involved are the men we've come to know—Peter, James, and John, Andrew, Nathanael, Bartholomew, Judas, and the others. How could this group of women travel as members of Jesus' band without raising eyebrows?

The gospel writers don't answer that question for us. What we do know is that while Jesus' enemies accused Him of Sabbath-breaking, of drinking too much wine, and of associating too closely with tax collectors and other disreputable types, at no time did they ever raise a question about sexual immorality. We must assume that these men and women traveled together in a way that avoided scandal.

First named among the women in that band was Mary Magdalene. We know nothing more about her background. Some commentators believe she came from a wealthy family and was thus able to help support Jesus and His other followers. That may or may not have been the case.

You may have heard of the musical stage show called

"Jesus Christ Superstar." In it Mary Magdalene was portrayed as a woman who practiced the "oldest profession on earth," prostitution. Yet in the Scripture we find no basis for that idea.

This myth about Mary Magdalene started in the sixth century when a pope named Gregory linked her with the sinful woman who anointed Jesus' feet with expensive perfumed oil. Ever since, throughout the past fourteen centuries artists have portrayed Mary Magdalene as a voluptuous hooker. Churches have named homes for rescued prostitutes as Magdalene houses. Despite the myth, Mary Magdalene was not a prostitute. Furthermore, we have no evidence that demon possession led to immorality in anyone's life. Demon possession doesn't produce sin.

The first two facts we know about Mary are that Jesus cast seven demons out of her and that she was a permanent part of the group that traveled with Him. The third thing the Bible tells us about Mary is that on a bad Friday called Good Friday she stayed at the cross long after the disciples had fled. From Mark we learn that "some women were watching from a distance. Among them were Mary Magdalene, Mary the mother of James the younger and of Joses, and Salome. In Galilee these women had followed Him and cared for his needs. Many other women who had come up with him to Jerusalem were also there" (Mark 15:40–41).

After three agonizing hours, Jesus died. Joseph of Arimathea, along with Nicodemus, came to take the body of Jesus off the cross and place it in a tomb. Matthew tells us that "Joseph took the body, wrapped it in a clean linen cloth, and placed it in his own new tomb that he had cut out of the rock. He rolled a big stone in

140

front of the entrance to the tomb and went away. Mary Magdalene and the other Mary were sitting across from the tomb" (Matthew 27:59–61).

All four gospel writers take pains to tell us that Mary and the other women not only stayed through the awful hours of crucifixion but made sure they knew where Jesus had been buried so they could come after the Sabbath and finish anointing the body. When we look at Mary Magdalene and the others, we see women who were completely committed to Jesus Christ even in the midst of their bitter grief.

It comes as no surprise that we find these same women, with Mary Magdalene apparently leading them, up before dawn on Sunday morning, hurrying to the garden tomb. Here were women carrying out their normal role in Jewish society, preparing a dead body for proper burial. As they went, they fretted about a very real problem they faced: who would roll away the large stone at the entrance to the tomb?

They knew the size of the stone. They had watched as Joseph and Nicodemus hastily laid Jesus' body in the tomb and rolled the heavy cartwheel across the opening. They also knew that the stone was sealed by the Roman government. That seal could not be broken. Yet they were determined to do the right thing for Jesus. They had cared for His needs for three years as He traveled around Galilee and back and forth to Judea. They had taken His physical well-being as their responsibility. So in His death they could not shrink from giving Him a correct burial. Despite the obstacles—a huge stone and a Roman seal—they seized the first opportunity to come to the tomb.

When they arrived, what did they find? Mark tells us

that "they saw that the stone, which was very large, had been rolled away" (Mark 16:4). In that moment began Mary's next lesson in discipleship. She had set out that morning with one set of expectations and quickly found them turned upside down. John reports the incident this way:

> Early on the first day of the week, while it was still dark, Mary Magdalene went to the tomb and saw that the stone had been removed from the entrance. So she came running to Simon Peter and the other disciple, the one Jesus loved, and said, "They have taken the Lord out of the tomb, and we don't know where they have put him!"
>
> So Peter and the other disciple started for the tomb. Both were running, but the other disciple outran Peter and reached the tomb first. He bent over and looked in at the strips of linen lying there but did not go in. Then Simon Peter, who was behind him, arrived and went into the tomb. He saw the strips of linen lying there, as well as the burial cloth that had been around Jesus' head. The cloth was folded up by itself, separate from the linen. Finally the other disciple, who had reached the tomb first, also went inside. He saw and believed. (They still did not understand from Scripture that Jesus had to rise from the dead.)
>
> Then the disciples went back to their homes, but Mary stood outside the tomb crying. As she wept, she bent over to look into the tomb and saw two angels in white, seated where Jesus' body had been, one at the head and the other at the foot. (20:1–11)

Mary, seeing the stone rolled away, made an assumption. She concluded that Jesus' body had been taken away and laid elsewhere. In that moment she could not think of Jesus as anything but dead. She had watched Him die. She had seen Him placed in this tomb.

Running to Peter and John, she followed them back to the tomb but stood outside weeping. This was the final blow. Enormous emotional tension had built up over the preceding weeks. Standing there she may have remembered that last trip from Galilee to Judea, that seventy-mile walk to Jerusalem. Among other things had been Jesus' ominous prediction of His coming death. But overshadowing that had been the thrill of Jesus' triumphal entry into Jerusalem. She had heard the adulation of the crowds crying out, "Hosanna to the Son of David! Blessed is he who comes in the name of the Lord! Hosanna in the highest!"

She had stood in the Court of the Women and watched as Jesus entered the temple and overturned the tables of the money-changers. She swelled with pride as He drove out evil men who were fleecing the poor pilgrims coming to the Holy City to celebrate the Passover. She held her breath, seeing the fury of the chief priests and Pharisees as Jesus taught for the last time in the temple courtyard.

She may have watched at the house of Simon the Leper as Mary of Bethany anointed Jesus. If so, she heard Him again predict His own death. She may have been present at Jesus' trial. We know she was there as He was led away to execution. She was there as the nails were driven into His hands and feet. She was there when the spear split open His side. She was there as the sky darkened at midday and a strong earthquake broke open rocks and graves. She had stood with the other women at the foot of the cross watching the one who had delivered her from seven demons now seemingly unable to deliver Himself. She watched Him die.

The highs and lows of that week all flowed together. She felt again the sting of contradiction as she remembered hearing crowds chant "Hosanna" one day and "Away with him! Crucify him!" only a few days later. Mary who had experienced that emotional roller-coaster now stood at the tomb, wrung out, devastated by the thought that, even in death, Jesus was violated. His body had been taken. Her wrenching sobs expressed all the dashed hopes and desperation she felt.

> Mary stood outside the tomb crying. As she wept, she bent over to look into the tomb and saw two angels in white, seated where Jesus' body had been, one at the head and the other at the foot.
> They aked her, "Woman, why are you crying?"
> "They have taken my Lord away," she said, "and I don't know where they have put him." At this, she turned around and saw Jesus standing there, but she did not realize that it was Jesus. (John 20:10–14)

When Mary and the other women had arrived at the tomb earlier that morning, she had sped off to find Peter and John. Meanwhile the others entered the tomb and met the angels who said:

> "Why do you look for the living among the dead? He is not here; he has risen! Remember

how he told to you, while he was still with you in Galilee: 'The Son of Man must be delivered into the hands of sinful men, be crucified and on the third day be raised again?' " (Luke 24:5–8)

But now the weeping Mary, who had missed those words the first time, did not wait for those words of hope when she saw the angels. Blinded by her grief, she turned away from them. As she turned, she saw a man standing nearby. He spoke exactly the same words she had just heard from the angels in John 20:15–18:

"Woman . . . why are you cryping? Who is it you are looking for?"

Thinking he was the gardener, she said, "Sir, if you have carried him away, tell me where you have put him, and I will get him."

Jesus said to her, "Mary."

She turned toward him and cried out in Aramaic, "Rabboni!" (which means Teacher).

Jesus said, "Do not hold on to me, for I have not yet returned to the Father. Go instead to my brothers and tell them, 'I am returning to my Father and your Father, to my God and your God.' "

Mary Magdalene went to the disciples with the news: "I have seen the Lord!" And she told them that he had said these things to her.

What did it take to move Mary from desolation to exultation, and to galvanize her for witness? Only one thing. Jesus spoke her name in a voice she knew, and it was enough.

The Good Shepherd called the name of this weeping sheep, Mary, and she knew His voice. Suddenly everything that had been all wrong was now all right. The one who had been dead was now alive. The one who had delivered her from seven demons was once again with her. In her ecstatic joy she flung her arms around Him. Jesus gently disengaged her clinging hold on His body and gave her a task: Go and tell my brothers. In a split second this disciple had moved from abject sorrow to euphoria: the Teacher is alive! Now she had work to do.

The fourth thing we know about Mary Magdalene is that she was sent by Jesus as the first witness to the resurrection. He commissioned her to tell His brothers the good news. She became, as Augustine called her, "an apostle to the apostles."

Mary's mental horizon had been fixed in the past. Her thoughts had been riveted on a dead body. Only the living Christ Himself could move her out of her focus on the past into the future. In the future she was to go and tell.

Mary Magdalene was not the only follower of Jesus who needed a changed focus. In the same chapter John recounts Jesus' encounter with another of His followers:

Now Thomas (called Didymus), one of the Twelve, was not with the disciples when Jesus came [on Easter evening]. So the other disciples told him, "We have seen the Lord!"

But he said to them, "Unless I see the nail marks in his hands and put my finger where the nails were, and put my hand into his side, I will not believe it."

A week later his disciples were in the house

again, and Thomas was with them. Though the doors were locked, Jesus came and stood among them and said, "Peace be with you!"

Then he said to Thomas, "Put your finger here; see my hands. Reach out your hand and put it into my side. Stop doubting and believe."

Thomas said to him, "My Lord and my God!"

Then Jesus told him, "Because you have seen me, you have believed; blessed are those who have not seen and yet have believed." (John 20:24–29)

In both cases Jesus made a special appearance to one of His followers—to Mary in the garden and to Thomas in the upper room with the locked door. Both Mary and Thomas had thought Jesus was dead. They were preoccupied with the Jesus of the past. Only the physical presence of Jesus would convince them otherwise.

These who had set their minds on what they could see or touch had to learn to worship and love by faith. They could not cling to Jesus' physical presence. They had to learn to relate to the Savior in a different way.

Mary knew Jesus' voice when He spoke her name. To her Jesus gave a commission: go and tell. To Thomas, who had refused to believe the testimony of the other disciples, He gave a gentle rebuke: you have believed because you have seen me. Blessed are those who have not seen and yet have believed.

When I was a child, my parents took me to church almost every time the doors were open. Our church had a strong evangelistic outreach. Every service closed with a public invitation to non-Christians to come to Christ. Each summer the church sponsored six weeks of tent meetings at which various evangelists preached every night. Over the years our family never missed a service. It was not surprising that at the age of eight I went forward in a tent meeting to ask Jesus to come into my life.

What was supposed to be a source of great peace, however, was for me a source of great torment. During the next ten years I was wretched. I was sure God had not heard my prayers and made me a part of His family. In listening to all the visiting preachers at our church, I had gotten the idea that I'd feel cleansed from sin if God had truly forgiven me. I didn't have any earth-shaking, shivery experiences like the ones the evangelists described as part of other people's conversions. For me that meant I was not yet a Christian.

As a child and then as a teenager, I agonized and prayed. I wanted the experience that would confirm for me that God had, indeed, forgiven me and made me His child. I didn't understand that there are "diff'rent strokes for diff'rent folks."

To some people come experiences like Mary's in the garden or like Thomas's in the upper room. To others of us comes the word Jesus spoke to Thomas: Blessed are they who have not seen anything spectacular and yet have believed. I began to understand this only dimly after my first year in college. Later experiences as a pastor's wife and as a missionary helped me see more clearly that God deals with each of us as individuals. He calls each of His sheep by name. He knows exactly what we need as we walk with Him.

That is what our discipleship is about. It means learning to believe whether or not we have tangible evidence to go on. It means learning to trust our sovereign, loving God to do what is best for us, whether He does it with some dramatic experience or with silence.

Mary Magdalene

How has God worked in your life? What have you learned about Him that makes a difference in your life? Where have you moved in your understanding of who God is and what He is doing in and through you? Your answers to such questions will tell you the shape of your discipleship.

Women as well as men were disciples of the Savior in Palestine two thousand years ago. They followed Him, listened to Him, learned from Him, ministered to Him. We don't have Jesus' physical presence among us to see and touch and help as they did. We have been asked to "walk by faith and not by sight." But our discipleship can be just as real as theirs. We have the Bible to guide us and the fellowship of other Christians to sustain us and correct us.

In school we moved along from learning addition to subtraction to the multiplication tables, then on to fractions, percentages, equations, and theorems. We learned them so we can now balance a checkbook, work in a bank, or become an astrophysicist. All of that learning was to good purpose.

Jesus, the Master Teacher, guides each of us in different ways to learn what we need to know. No two of us have the same life experience. He takes us where we are and works with us there, but always to the same purpose. He wants to move us from ignorance of God to acquaintance to a deep relationship as His daughters. He moves us from no faith to faith to an unshakable confidence in the living God. He teaches us to see tough times as God's way of moving us to new ways of thinking about ourselves and our purpose in life. We walk with God each day as learners so that we can distinguish good from evil. We go on to maturity.

Questions for personal reflection or group discussion:

1. Mary Magdalene saw Jesus and heard Him call her name before she recognized Him. How can you recognize the living Christ today?
2. What does it mean to "walk by faith and not by sight"?
3. As you look at yourself as a learner in the hands of the Master Teacher, Jesus Christ, what experiences has He used to encourage you and teach you to keep on following Him?
4. What goals would you like to set for your discipleship as a Christian woman in the last decade of the twentieth century?

Note to the Reader

The publisher invites you to share your response to the message of this book by writing Discovery House Publishers, Box 3566, Grand Rapids, MI 49501, USA. For information about other Discovery House books, music, or videos, contact us at the same address or call 1-800-653-8333. Find us on the Internet at http://www.dhp.org/ or send e-mail to books@dhp.org.